First Coastal Californians

First Coastal

Edited by Lynn H. Gamble

with a foreword by Brian Fagan

Californians

School for Advanced Research Popular Archaeology Book

School for Advanced Research Press
Santa Fe

SAR
PRESS

School for Advanced Research Press
Post Office Box 2188
Santa Fe, New Mexico 87504-2188
www.sarpress.org

Managing Editor: Sarah Soliz
Editorial Assistant: Ellen Goldberg
Designer and Production Manager: Cynthia Dyer
Manuscript Editor: Jane Kepp
Proofreader: Sarah Soliz
Indexer: Margaret Moore Booker
Printed by Four Colour Print Group in South Korea

Library of Congress Cataloging-in-Publication Data

First coastal Californians / edited by Lynn H. Gamble. — First edition.
pages cm. — (School for Advanced Research popular archaeology book)
Includes bibliographical references and index.
ISBN 978-1-938645-19-8 (pbk.)
1. Indians of North America—California—History.
2. Indians of North America—California—Social life and customs.
3. Indians of North America—California—Antiquities. I. Gamble, Lynn H.
E78.C15F55 2015
979.4'00497—dc23
2015016602

© 2015 by the School for Advanced Research

Cover photograph: Chumash paintings at Pleito Creek, California, courtesy Rick Bury, photographer.

Frontispiece: Point Reyes National Seashore, California, courtesy Macduff Everton, photographer.

Contents

Color plates follow p. 46

Foreword

Brian Fagan

No three-story pueblos, no gold artifacts, no lavishly adorned chieftains buried in splendor commemorate thirteen thousand years of human life along the California coast. Yet researchers are discovering there a rich and eventful—if often ignored—history, manifested in shell mounds, buried villages, rock paintings, ancient fishhooks, and countless mollusk shells. Along the Pacific Ocean, California's first people thrived in an abundant yet challenging Middle World, the domain of the living sandwiched between the supernatural realms of the Lower and Upper Worlds. Theirs was a realm of sudden climatic shifts, of prolonged droughts and epochal rainstorms, of great abundance and chronic scarcities. Seemingly against all odds, some of the most complex hunter-gatherer societies on earth flourished along California's rugged, indented coastline.

Except for stories passed down by Native people over the centuries and some descriptions by colonists and early anthropologists, nearly everything we know of these remarkable societies—and they were remarkable—comes from archaeological research and, increasingly and encouragingly, multidisciplinary inquiry. Even if coastal archaeological sites are largely unspectacular, the results of research since the early twentieth century are truly fascinating, though little known outside archaeological circles. *First Coastal Californians* brings together an impressive group of experts to tell the story in a book aimed firmly at non-specialist readers.

This is a historical story wrought in stone artifacts, rare organic objects, and food remains—tiny fragments of the past that researchers piece together into a reasoned tale. But today's archaeologists venture far beyond mere artifacts and bones. Working closely with scientists from many other disciplines, they use the latest high-technology tools to unravel minute details of the coastal past. We now have a mine of information on ancient DNA, on large- and small-scale climate changes, on people's seasonal foraging, and on interpretations of rock art, to mention but a few striking discoveries. Today, archaeologists working on the California coast stand at the forefront of innovative research into the remote and not-so-remote past.

The California coast is no uniform environment. Rather, it is a collection of very diverse landscapes, everything from near desert to great estuaries, tidal flats, and precipitous cliffs. Some places, such as the San Francisco Bay area and the Santa Barbara Channel, were so rich in fish, sea mammals, and shellfish that pre-Columbian people could settle in the same locations for generations, even millennia. On those landscapes, the first Californians grew into dense populations living in small, circumscribed territories. Where land and sea were sparsely endowed, such as along much of the northern California shoreline, people remained sparse, too.

Yet for every Native group, survival depended in considerable part on interdependency and constant interactions with neighbors near and far. There was no such thing as a self-sufficient society along the California coast. Using new methods such as trace element analysis to identify the geographical sources of artifacts, researchers are revealing both regular and sporadic contacts between people living on offshore islands and on mainland shores and people living far in the interior. These interactions became so intense in later times that some kinds of shell beads became actual money, used over a large part of the central and southern coast.

Such interactions, especially trade, are among the central themes of this book. So are watercraft, which assumed important roles in coastal societies, whether for hunting sea mammals along exposed coasts or for fishing in great estuary areas like San Francisco Bay. The planked Chumash *tomol* is one of the best understood of all Native American watercraft, known to us from rare archaeological finds, from anthropologist John P. Harrington's memorable researches, and from voyages made to the Channel Islands in modern-day replicas. Here, we learn how the modest tule reed canoe was also vitally important at times when lower sea levels brought the offshore islands closer to the mainland.

Above all, this is a story of cultural continuity in the face of constant adjustments to droughts and other climatic events. People responded by moving or by settling in larger villages, and often they developed more complex societies in the process. But the basic pattern of coastal life never changed. Always Native Californians relied on inshore fishing, on harvesting mollusks, on hunting game at sea mammal rookeries, and on game and plant foods, especially acorns. Their story is one of brilliant adaptations to ever-changing, intensely challenging environments.

Those adaptations would have continued indefinitely had it not been for European exploration and settlement. The devastation caused by the newcomers is rightly described here in two important chapters as a "cultural earthquake," a tsunami of disease, violence, and cultural and social upheaval. Rightly, too, the book ends with an essay by a Rumsien Ohlone descendant who has resurrected the basket-making artistry of her ancestors. Her story is a powerful reminder of the resilience and continuity of the First People.

First Coastal Californians is an authoritative and important book honoring humans' first thirteen thousand years of life along the Pacific coast. Its authors eloquently tell a little-known story in words unburdened by the jargon of modern-day archaeology. A broad constituency of readers will enjoy these pages— not only archaeologists and students but also Native Californians and general readers. There is abundant food for thought here, and a wonderful achievement: the recounting of an important chapter in early American history for everyone to enjoy.

A Chronology of Coastal California Indian History

Dates are given as BCE ("before the common era") and CE ("of the common era")

Climatic Periods and Geological Events

9000 BCE   End of the Pleistocene epoch and the last ice age; beginning of the Holocene epoch.

9000–5500 BCE   Early Holocene. Sea level rises; flooding of some coastal lowlands and canyons.

5500–1500 BCE   Middle Holocene. Generally warmer and drier than Early Holocene; sea level stabilizes between 6,000 and 5,000 years ago.

1500 BCE–present Late Holocene. Environmental conditions roughly similar to those of today.

1000–1250 CE   Medieval climatic anomaly. Extended droughts and warmer temperatures in some regions.

Cultural Periods and Events

11,500–8000 BCE   Paleoindian era. Clovis culture widespread across North America between 11,050 and 10,800 BCE.

11,000 BCE   Arlington Man dies on Santa Rosa Island; pygmy mammoths become extinct on the northern Channel Islands.

9500 BCE   Sea-oriented foragers first live at Daisy Cave on San Miguel Island.

8000–3500 BCE   Early Archaic period, also known as the Milling Stone culture, in central California.

5500–600 BCE   Early Period in southern California. People are relatively mobile, but a few settlements grow large and more permanent.

3500–600 BCE   Early Period in central California. People are relatively mobile; hunting increases in significance.

600 BCE–1150 CE   Middle Period in southern California. Larger settlements; populations less mobile; evidence of shell bead making on northern Channel Islands.

600 BCE–1000 CE   Middle Period in central California. Hunting and fishing increase; large shell mounds are used intensively around San Francisco Bay.

500 CE   Clear archaeological evidence of plank canoes in southern California.

1150–1782 CE   Late Period in southern California. Large, permanently occupied coastal settlements with heavy reliance on marine resources.

1250–1769 CE   Late Period in central California. Greater sedentism.

1542 CE   Juan Rodríguez Cabrillo sails to coastal California, becoming its first known non-Native visitor.

1579 CE   Sir Francis Drake lands somewhere around Drake's Bay in today's Marin County.

1602–1603 CE   Sebastián Vizcaino sails along the California coast.

1769 CE   First Spanish land expedition, led by Gaspar de Portolá, enters California looking for suitable mission sites between San Diego and Monterey Bay. Mission San Diego de Alcalá and San Diego Presidio are established.

1775 CE   Ipai and Tipai attack Mission San Diego.

1781–1823 CE   Pueblo de Los Angeles founded 1781; additional missions and presidios established between 1782 and 1823.

1824 CE   Chumash uprising at Missions Santa Inés, Santa Barbara, and La Purísima.

1835–1836 CE   Missions are secularized, and their properties become private ranchos.

1848 CE   Treaty of Guadalupe Hidalgo ends Mexican-American war; California annexed to the United States.

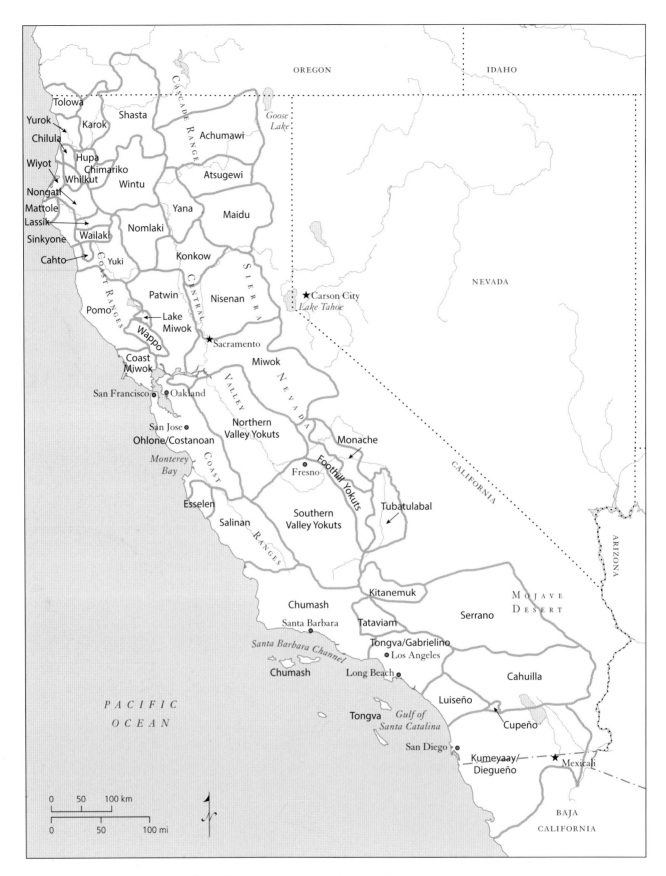

Major Native language groups of the California culture area at the time of European contact.

First Coastal Californians

Figure 1.1. A Pomo Indian woman gathering seeds with a seed beater and basket, date unknown. Today, speakers of the Pomo languages live along the California coast north of San Francisco Bay, in some of the same places in which their ancestors lived.

Thirteen Thousand Years on the Coast

Lynn H. Gamble

It is the year 1312 in a place people now call California. A small group of Chumash Indian leaders—a few chiefs, an astronomer, a messenger, a master of herbs, a curing doctor—huddle around the fire in a sweat lodge at Syuxtun, a Pacific coast village overlooking islands in the Santa Barbara Channel. For these men, the place is the Middle World, the center of the universe and the world in which the First People live. The Middle World lies between the feared Lower World, filled with malevolent beings, and the respected Upper World, where powerful Sky People control the heavens.

Suddenly, the men in the lodge feel a jolt. The earth shakes and rumbles. One chief remarks that the two giant serpents holding up the Middle World must be tired. From time to time the serpents performing this vital job grow weary and need to shift, causing earthquakes.

The Middle World is the setting, too, for the story my colleagues and I tell in this book. From north of San Francisco Bay to south of San Diego, a landscape teeming with food beckoned to some of the first humans to set foot in North America and nourished their descendants for more than twelve thousand years. The shoreline of the Pacific served up a rich variety of fish, shellfish, and sea mammals. Around the adjacent bays and lagoons and in the surrounding foothills, people could hunt land mammals and collect acorns, seeds, roots, and bulbs. Tumbling down the foothills and across the coastal terraces, creeks and rivers teemed with fish.

So abundant were all these wild sources of food

that Indians of the California coast, unlike their counterparts in most of the rest of North America, never had to take up farming. By the time the first Spaniards arrived on the coast in 1542, California Indians had developed flourishing, socially complex societies supported entirely by hunting, gathering, and fishing. Although these people never built large stone or adobe houses like those of the southwestern Pueblo Indians, or great stone pyramids, as some Mexican Indians did, they created far-reaching, thriving networks of trade and social interrelationships.

The story begins with early seafarers who landed on California's northern Channel Islands (chapter 2). On Santa Rosa Island, a lone skeleton protruding from the steep banks of a canyon caught the eye of archaeologist Phil Orr in 1959. Recent analyses and radiocarbon dating of the bones, known to researchers

Figure 1.2. Ohlone Indian dancers with painted bodies at Mission San José, at the southern tip of San Francisco Bay, 1806. Lithograph based on a sketch by W. G. T. von Tilenau.

as Arlington Man, show that the bones date to about thirteen thousand years ago, near the end of the Pleistocene geological epoch. They are the earliest evidence so far of humans living in California, and among the earliest cases in all the Americas.

Thirteen thousand years ago, the environment and coastlines of California were very different from those of today. The man who died at Arlington Springs lived on a "super-island" known as Santarosae, which formed during the last ice age, when sea levels were much lower than they are now (chapter 3). Woolly mammoths and their smaller pygmy mammoth cousins still roamed the island, right before their extinction. Despite the lower sea levels, the only way people could have arrived on Santarosae was by boat. The early dates for Arlington Man and for other archaeological sites on the northern Channel Islands challenge the once widely believed idea that the first humans to enter the Americas came by foot over the Bering Strait land bridge. Perhaps instead, or in addition, they found their way to the Americas by boat.

From thirteen thousand years ago, jump ahead 11,231 years. It is 1769, and Spanish soldiers are marching up from Baja California to the San Francisco Bay, looking for good places to establish missions and forts (chapter 14). Everywhere they meet residents of different local cultures. Each group wears a distinctive style of clothing, unique accoutrements, and special symbols tattooed across bodies and faces. The groups speak many different languages (see map page x), but they are all interconnected through a web of trade. Most of them happily treat their foreign visitors to opulent feasts accompanied by music, dancing, and gifts. Chiefs emerge bedecked in their finest to deliver speeches, showing respect for their visitors (chapter 10). They hand out shell beads and baskets filled with food. The beads are especially valuable, for it takes tremendous effort to make these tiny ornaments. Many of them are so small that today they pass right through the window screens that archaeologists use as sieves.

The coastal California seen by European explorers (plate 10) had changed greatly from the place where seafarers first landed thousands of years before. Sea

Figure 1.3. Two California Indian women from the San Francisco Bay area, wearing tule reed skirts, a feather cape (*left*), and a deerskin robe (*right*). Hand-colored engraving from an 1816 drawing by Louis Choris, artist for a Russian expedition under Lt. Otto von Kotzebue.

levels had risen nearly 250 feet as the planet thawed after the last ice age, dramatically altering coastlines, rivers, and wetlands and the plants and animals they offered to humans. A formerly open bay in the Pacific Ocean near modern Los Angeles, for example, had become a lagoon hosting masses of waterfowl (chapter 9).

Just as important, the landscape had filled with people over the centuries as waves of Native immigrants moved in. Linguists have been able to trace the relative timing of some of these migrations. They know, for instance, that the Chumash language family, which is not demonstrably related to other California Indian languages, has deep roots in the area around Santa Barbara. Its speakers must have been among the earliest to arrive. Over time, linguistic diversity throughout California increased, and some Indian groups moved into the coastal strip fairly late.

Altogether, California Indians spoke roughly eighty languages. In some places along the coast, speakers of different tongues lived as close neighbors, side by side in small regions. A Coast Miwok person from the San Francisco Bay area who traveled a hundred miles from home might have heard people speaking twenty languages or more. Although few California Indians traveled widely, many of those living

Figure 1.4. Earth-covered houses and acorn granaries at the Konkow Indian village of Céno, on the banks of the Sacramento River, about 1850. Pencil and ink wash by Henry B. Brown, 1851–1852.

in border areas probably spoke at least two languages. Looking a little farther inland to the Wintu Indians, we know that some shamans could switch from one language to another when channeling spirits.

For thousands of years after the first seafarers landed on California shores, while the sea slowly rose and newcomers trickled in, Native people along the coast tended to live fairly similar lives. In small bands of a few related families apiece, they moved frequently about the landscape, following game animals and ripening plants as they came into season. On the coast they fished, hunted sea mammals, and collected shellfish. Inland they gathered large quantities of small seeds in expertly made baskets, later grinding the seeds into flour with stone milling tools. Wherever they camped for a while, they built brush huts and left behind the animal bones and broken tools that today signal archaeological sites.

Eventually, by about five thousand years ago, after sea level had stabilized at roughly its present level, human populations in many parts of coastal California had grown large enough that bands could no longer move so freely over the land. Former seasonal campsites and hamlets now became villages where people lived year-round. Settlements also began to look

increasingly different in areas along the coast from north to south (chapters 6–9).

Around San Francisco Bay, villagers about thirty-eight hundred years ago started building up imposing shell mounds, which rose ever higher over the millennia as mourners buried in them their dead and the detritus of funeral feasts (chapter 6). Later, people also lived on the mounds in tightly packed villages of small, earth-covered houses and larger dance houses. Using ingenious fish weirs, or dams—some so large that several people could walk abreast on top of them—these early Bay Area residents caught millions of salmon and other spawning fish, many of which they smoked and dried to eat later. Chiefs staged great feasts at fish-harvesting time, inviting other chiefs and commoners from surrounding settlements to enjoy the catch in exchange for shell beads. Today, few of the mounds remain; Euroamericans destroyed most of them in the late nineteenth and early twentieth centuries for farming and urban development. Yet new studies of collections made by pioneering archaeologists and new work in surviving remnants of mounds are yielding fresh and sometimes surprising understandings of the mound dwellers' lives.

South of the Bay Area, along the central coast,

Figure 1.5. Excavations by a crew led by Lynn Gamble at an archaeological site on Santa Cruz Island. Ancestral Chumash people lived there from about six thousand to twenty-five hundred years ago.

California Indians began to cluster around estuaries and in adjacent valleys about ten thousand years ago. There they fished, gathered shellfish, hunted small animals, and collected wild plant seeds (chapter 7). So ubiquitous in archaeological sites are the flat milling stones on which people ground seeds into flour that archaeologists call their way of life the "Milling Stone" culture. This lifestyle endured for some forty-five hundred years, only to disappear at a time of cooler climate and new immigration into the region. Replacing it about fifty-five hundred years ago came a lifestyle founded on hunting larger game, collecting and grinding acorns, and, increasingly, fishing—especially after the invention of a new, more efficient style of fishhook about three thousand years ago. Hunters, too, benefited from innovation when the bow and arrow quickly caught on about fifteen hundred years ago. By the time the first Spanish land expedition, under Gaspar de Portolá, arrived in 1769, Native groups speaking at least seven languages lived in small villages on the central coast, making use of an enormous variety of natural resources in ways finely honed over hundreds of generations.

In contrast to the central coast, with its many language groups living side by side, the next place on our north-to-south tour was home for at least the last seventy-five hundred years to people from a single language family, Chumash (chapter 8). The stretch of coast along the Santa Barbara Channel, protected from large surf by the offshore Channel Islands, provided calm waters for early fishing boats and sustained a rich marine life. Today, the channel supports one of the most prolific coastal fisheries in the world, partly because of its geographical situation and the upward movement of nutrient-rich deep water. Seaweeds and phytoplankton thrive, a veritable banquet for marine fish. Sea mammals living in the channel's kelp beds dine on the fish, and Chumash people throughout pre-Columbian times dined on both. They fished and hunted from sewn plank canoes, a novel type of watercraft found nowhere else in North America (chapter 5).

Figure 1.6. Carved soapstone effigies of fish and other creatures from a site at Malibu, California. Such talismans or amulets reflected Native spiritual beliefs.

a habitat rich in shellfish, birds, and small mammals, highly attractive to humans. People began to settle more permanently in the area, in villages instead of hunting camps. They hunted aquatic birds, fished, and gathered abundant oysters and clams. They buried their dead and conducted mourning ceremonies along the edges of the lagoon, practices they continued even after Spanish colonization began to upend their way of life forever.

Wherever they lived along the coast, California Indians, like people everywhere throughout human history, faced challenges posed by unpredictable weather and climate: lengthy droughts, catastrophic floods, changing sea temperatures, and El Niño events. In response, they developed ways to manage their environment for the greatest food security possible (chapter 4). One of the best examples is their deliberate burning of the terrain. Today, disastrous fires plague Californians, obliterating not only forests but also entire human communities. California Indians developed a different relationship with fire: they used it to their advantage, as a tool to enhance the diversity of resources on which they relied. By intentionally setting fire to an area—rather the way the US Forest Service now conducts "prescribed burns" to thin underbrush—Native people created conditions that favored the growth of new plants and tender shoots to be used for food and materials for housing, cooking utensils, storage containers, weapons, baskets, and other basics of daily survival.

But California Indians' lives were not only about the necessities. They were also rich in religious observances filled with celebratory feasting, dancing, and singing. Secret religious societies, composed of the elites of the community, regularly held ceremonies and initiation rites in which girls and boys learned how to handle the dangerous power contained in the group's

The channel coast was also known for its shell bead makers, who spent countless hours hunched over stone anvils shaping and drilling small seashells into beads (chapter 12; plate 5). Some kinds of shell beads belonged only to chiefs and other high-status persons, but other kinds served as money, available to many people for paying debts, buying food, purchasing dance regalia, procuring services, and acquiring brides. Like the Chumash, most other California Indians relied on shell beads as indispensable objects in daily life.

Just south of the Santa Barbara Channel, near where Los Angeles International Airport now sits, Indians once lived in lush wetlands around Ballona Creek, the original main course of the Los Angeles River. Now largely drained and covered by the industrial and residential buildings of west Los Angeles, the area called "the Ballona" still holds surprisingly plentiful traces of a successful Native way of life. Excavating in the heart of the city, archaeologists have investigated eight thousand years of human residence there (chapter 9). At first, families visited the shores of an open bay on the Pacific to fish and hunt for a week or two at a time. As sea level rose and then stabilized, the open coast at Ballona became a lagoon, ceremonial paraphernalia (chapter 11). Membership in the secret societies buttressed the elites' political and social power, and members' performances of both secret and public ceremonies reinforced the legitimacy of chiefs and other leaders. Public ritual celebrations often brought many commoners together, too, to visit with friends and relatives, exchange beads and food, and meet potential marriage partners.

Far removed from such ritual gatherings, people left hints of an entirely different aspect of religious life. Painted on remote rocks in the backcountry are all sorts of images—in some areas, myriad spiders, turtles, coyotes, bears, condors, lizards, salamanders, water striders, and frogs; in others, winged dancers, brilliant sunlike images, and streaking comets. Produced by shamans, astronomers, and other experts entrusted with maintaining cosmic equilibrium in an uncertain world, these images mark places of power, mystery, and self-induced trances. Although pre-Columbian Indians had no writing in the sense in which we know it today, they depicted their spiritual lives and cosmic beliefs on stone. Archaeologists recognize these images as some of the most spectacular rock art in the world, and specialists continue to document these hidden places and interpret their meanings (chapter 13).

It is hard not to wonder what life might be like for California Indians today if Europeans had never stepped ashore in the Middle World. But step ashore they did, and we will never know, for example, whether the many language groups would have stayed separate and distinct or might have melded over time, or whether coastal people would ever have begun growing maize like their neighbors in the Southwest. After several hundred years of exploration, Spaniards colonized coastal California, establishing powerful institutions—especially Catholic missions backed up by military forts—that changed the lives of the first Californians forever (chapters 14–16). The newcomers brought with them an onslaught of disease, the curtailment of traditional hunting and gathering grounds, unhealthy living conditions in dank mission barracks, and countless hours of forced labor.

Yet California Indians did not simply succumb to the colonizers. Rebellion, resistance, cooperation, and persistence are all threads in the story of this period of stunning change. Native people survived, and today they thrive. One hallmark of California Indian culture, the basket, is still woven today from the same materials employed for thousands of years, gathered in the same woods and meadows (chapter 17). Collectors prize these baskets highly, just as did early Spanish, Portuguese, English, French, Russian, and American voyagers, who competed to acquire the finest baskets to send back home (plate 1). In 1775 and 1776, when the Anza expedition passed through southern California, its men bought so many baskets that subsequent travelers complained that few were left for them to purchase.

With the signing of the Treaty of Guadalupe Hidalgo in 1848, Mexico ceded the territories of California, New Mexico, and Arizona to the United States. Disastrously for California Indians, in the same year the treaty was signed a white man discovered gold near present-day Sacramento, sparking the United States' first gold rush. Euroamericans swarmed into central California seeking fortunes; only a year later, an estimated one hundred thousand miners lived in California. Single-mindedly ruthless in their quest for gold, miners massacred California Indian men, women, and children if they stood in the way. Those who were spared found themselves dispossessed of their traditional land and, in many cases, enslaved. Without women companions, miners freely raped Indian women. Some researchers have estimated that only two years after the gold strike, one hundred thousand California Indians had died.

Passage of the Homestead Act in 1862, which offered vast tracts of land cheap to white settlers, attracted even more land-hungry immigrants to displace even more Native Californians. With so many Indians dead or displaced, rituals and traditions deteriorated along with the food-producing environment. By 1870, perhaps as few as fifty thousand California Indians still lived.

Finally, in the late nineteenth and early twentieth centuries, the US government began to establish federally recognized reservations and rancherias for California Indians. Many Native groups living near the coast, however, never received federal recognition, partly because the coastal strip had been colonized so early by whites and its original residents had already been displaced or mixed together for several centuries. Native people in this region still struggle for the rights and recognition afforded to some other Indians in the state and throughout the nation.

Despite the devastation of the Spanish, Mexican, and early American years, some California Indian populations have rebounded from their lowest ebb. Tribal members work to ensure that traditional customs such as basket weaving and the building of plank canoes continue to flourish or are revived. They have successfully saved some of their traditional plant-collecting areas and ancestral burial grounds. California Indian lawyers, environmental specialists, engineers, teachers, and scientists work with traditional specialists and others to maintain group identities and deep cultural values. It is a testimony to the resilience of California Indians that they thrive today, dancing in the footsteps of their ancestors.

Figure 2.1. California sea lions swimming in kelp beds near Anacapa Island, California.

The Kelp Highway and the First Californians

Jon M. Erlandson and Torben C. Rick

Just off the California coast, out of sight of the millions of vacationers drawn every year to the state's beautiful sand beaches and rocky shores, lie enormous kelp beds that form the canopies of towering ocean forests. In these forests thrive a multitude of animals and plants—seaweeds, seals, shellfish, seabirds, sharks and other fish. After paralleling California coastlines for nearly a thousand miles, the prolific kelp forests continue northward off the shores of Oregon, Washington, British Columbia, and Alaska, all the way to Kamchatka and northern Japan. They offered a rich larder to some of the first humans to reach North America. In effect, they formed a "kelp highway" that people traveled by boat during a coastal migration spanning centuries or even millennia.

Just a decade or so ago, most archaeologists considered such a migration improbable. Now many researchers believe that a coastal route around the Pacific Rim was the most likely way humans journeyed from northeast Asia to the Americas. Studies of human DNA samples suggest that this journey took place fifteen thousand to seventeen thousand years ago, near the end of the Pleistocene geological epoch, when the waning of the last ice age caused climates to warm and glaciers to recede from Pacific Northwest coastlines.

For most of the twentieth century, no archaeological sites along the Pacific coast yielded widely accepted Late Pleistocene dates. This led most scholars to think the Americas were first colonized about thirteen thousand years ago by terrestrial hunting people who migrated across a broad land bridge known as

Beringia, which connected northeast Asia and North America during the last glacial period. These people, whom archaeologists christened "Paleoindians," then walked down a long, narrow, ice-free corridor through what is now Canada, emerging onto the Great Plains as the Clovis culture. Only later did their descendants spread from sea to shining sea, with seafaring and fishing cultures developing long after Clovis times. The California coast played no significant role in this "Clovis first" theory, which scholars ardently defended for decades but which has now collapsed like a house of cards.

Across the Pacific, evidence that seafaring people settled islands off the East Asian coast between fifty thousand and fifteen thousand years ago helped turn the tide in favor of a coastal migration. Then, a discovery at a waterlogged campsite near the coast of Chile sank the Clovis first model. Excavators there found several types of kelp and seaweed together with stone tools, all roughly fourteen thousand years old— before the fabled ice-free corridor is thought to have opened up.

How did people reach central Chile before the ice-free corridor opened? A coastal route, entirely at sea level and rich in food sources, offered no major obstacles to maritime people and appears to have been passable by at least sixteen thousand years ago. Around the Pacific Rim, rising postglacial seas created productive estuaries, perfect "rest stops" for migrating coastal folk. Some of the estuaries sit at the mouths of large rivers such as the Fraser, Columbia, Klamath, and Sacramento, where salmon and other fish ran in huge numbers. These rivers and fisheries might have beckoned as detours that some early coastal people followed deep into the interior of western North America. The climate was wetter then than it is today, so the migrants' coastal lifestyles could easily have been adapted to large lakes and marshes in California's Central Valley and in the Great Basin.

Science involves hypotheses and theories, but testing the coastal migration theory is challenging because global sea levels have risen roughly four hundred feet since the end of the last glaciation. The ocean has drowned the shorelines early coastal people would have followed from Asia to the Americas, along with a miles-wide swath of coastal lowlands. If the earliest coastal sites lie submerged on continental shelves, how can archaeologists test the kelp highway hypothesis? Underwater archaeology may be the key, but it is difficult and expensive, especially in deep waters. We have reconstructed ancient landscapes along the Pacific coast and dabbled in some underwater work, but most of our efforts have taken place on land, especially on California's Channel Islands.

On these relatively arid islands, which receive little or no rainfall for six months of the year, we identified and searched geographical features that drew early maritime people into the interiors of the islands. We paid special attention to caves and rock shelters, freshwater springs, outcrops of chert used to make stone tools, and elevated landforms with commanding views. Over the past twenty-plus years, we have found more than a dozen archaeological sites where maritime Paleoindians, also known as Paleocoastal Indians, lived between about 12,200 and 10,000 years ago. Recent research at the earliest of these sites tells a remarkable story about the lives of some of the first Americans, who took much of their food from the kelp forests and coastal fisheries.

California's eight Channel Islands form southern and northern groups. The southern islands—San Clemente, Santa Catalina, San Nicolas, and Santa Barbara—have been separate and relatively remote for tens of thousands of years. The northern islands—Anacapa, Santa Cruz, Santa Rosa, and San Miguel—cluster tightly off the Santa Barbara coast. Now lying between thirteen and twenty-seven miles from the mainland, the northern islands were merged into a single, larger island known as Santarosae until about

Figure 2.2. The outline of former Santarosae Island, encompassing the current Channel Islands of (west to east) San Miguel, Santa Rosa, Santa Cruz, and Anacapa, before sea level rose over the past twenty thousand years.

ten thousand years ago, when rising seas flooded the coastal lowlands between them (chapter 3). Between about twenty thousand and thirteen thousand years ago, the east end of Santarosae was separated from the mainland by a strait only four to six miles wide, but strong currents sweeping through this narrow channel may have made it difficult to navigate.

Before Europeans introduced livestock and other animals, the Channel Islands had few land mammals. Wooly mammoths and their diminutive pygmy cousins roamed the northern islands until about thirteen thousand years ago, but after their demise the only sizable land mammals were dogs, foxes, and skunks, all of which may have been introduced by Native Americans. It is still unclear whether the island mammoths fell victim to human hunters, to shrinking island habitat, or to both.

What the islands did have was a wealth of marine animals that fed in the vast offshore forests of giant kelp and bull kelp. To reproduce, kelp plants release billions of tiny spores that fuel rich, complex food webs. Modeling of ancient coastal habitats around the northern islands suggests that the first islanders saw kelp forests considerably more extensive than today's. Without large terrestrial predators until humans arrived on the scene, Santarosae was probably a refuge for huge numbers of seals and sea lions, seabirds and migratory waterfowl. Tens of thousands of whales, dolphins, and porpoises swimming through island waters added to the bounty available to early islanders. Not only that, but the recovery of island plant communities after a century of heavy grazing

Figure 2.3. Phil Orr's excavation at the Arlington Springs site on Santa Rosa Island, 1959. At the bottom of an ancient arroyo, Orr found the bones of Arlington Man, which date to about thirteen thousand years ago.

is revealing that edible plants on the Channel Islands were much more abundant than previously imagined.

Once thought to have been marginal habitat in comparison with the mainland, the islands now seem to have been a magnet for early maritime people. The earliest known archaeological site on the islands, and one of the most important, is Arlington Springs on Santa Rosa Island. There, in 1959, Phil Orr of the Santa Barbara Museum of Natural History (SBMNH) found three leg bones from a human now known as Arlington Man eroding from an ancient arroyo, thirty-seven feet below the modern ground surface. After insisting for years that natural "fire areas" dating to forty thousand years ago were the work of humans who hunted and cooked mammoths on the

island—an idea most scholars rejected—Orr had little credibility with other archaeologists. At Arlington Springs he used a newly developed carbon dating technique to estimate the age of the human bones at ten thousand radiocarbon years ago, roughly a thousand years younger than Clovis sites in the interior of North America.

More recently, meticulous dating and stratigraphic work led by John Johnson, one of Orr's successors at the SBMNH, has shown that Arlington Man died about thirteen thousand calendar years ago, a corrected radiocarbon age that is contemporary with Clovis. This places seafaring Paleoindians on Santarosae at the same time Clovis hunters chased mammoths on the Great Plains. Because no tools, clothing, or food refuse were found with Arlington Man, his relationship to Clovis people and his lifestyle remain poorly known.

During the 1990s, on San Miguel Island, we excavated a thin layer of dark soil at an archaeological site called Daisy Cave that held small amounts of marine shell and a handful of stone artifacts dating to about 11,600 years ago. This buried cultural layer, first identified by Pandora Snethkamp and Dan Guthrie, yielded several types of shellfish associated with kelp forests, including red abalone, mussel, black turban snail, and chiton. Above this was a thicker soil layer dating between 10,000 and 8,600 years ago, which produced an amazing assemblage of woven sea grass artifacts, stone points and knives, a chipped stone crescent, shell beads, small bone fish-hooks, shellfish remains, marine mammal bones, and thousands of fish bones from kelp forests and rocky nearshore habitats.

A few years later, again on San Miguel Island, we identified a large Paleocoastal site complex at Cardwell Bluffs, where chert cobbles lay exposed on the surface of a large eroded area high above the seacoast. Five shell middens, or refuse deposits, in the site complex date between about 12,200 and 11,400 years ago. They are the oldest known shell middens along the Pacific coast of North America, and they contain the same types of shellfish found in the oldest layer at Daisy Cave. The thousands of stone artifacts we uncovered at Cardwell Bluffs make it clear that these sites were combined quarries, workshops, and campsites where Paleocoastal people flaked chert cobbles into projectile points, knives, and other tools.

Especially striking among the artifacts are distinctive chipped stone crescents and delicate "stemmed" points. Clearly part of a sophisticated maritime hunting and fishing technology, the crescents and stemmed points resemble artifacts found in early archaeological sites in the Great Basin, on the Columbia Plateau, and in California's Central Valley. But on an island lacking large terrestrial game, what were they used for?

The answer to that question came from the

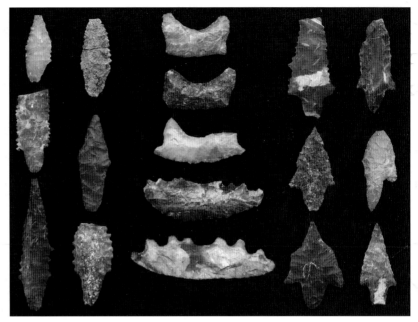

Figure 2.4. Paleocoastal chipped stone artifacts from the Cardwell Bluffs sites on San Miguel Island. *Left*: stemmed points of a type called the Channel Island Amol point; *center*: crescents; *right*: Channel Island Barbed points. The large crescent at bottom center is 2.9 inches long.

discovery and excavation of two sites located near Arlington Springs on Santa Rosa Island. Exposed deep in eroding sea cliffs and arroyos, these sites were challenging to dig, but our efforts were rewarded with remarkable discoveries that have changed our understanding of the maritime lifestyles of some of the earliest Californians. In a dark and deeply buried soil at a site known as CA-SRI-512, we found thousands of bones from seabirds, migratory geese, fish, and marine mammals, along with crescents, points, and other artifacts dated to about 11,750 years ago. The bones from migratory geese suggest that people camped at the site during the late fall or winter, when they harvested birds, seals, fish, and shellfish from nearby marshes and from the coast, several miles away. Most of the tools are made from local island rocks, but a small flake of obsidian shows that early islanders had trade connections with mainland tribes deep in the interior, beyond the southern Sierra Nevada, who lived near sources of this volcanic glass.

We recently found several more sites on Santa Rosa Island that Paleocoastal people used between about 12,200 and 11,000 years ago. Preliminary work at these sites has turned up similar tools and animal remains. Clamshells found at one site show that early

Figure 2.5. A finely crafted Channel Island Amol point from CA-SRI-26, an 11,600-year-old site on Santa Rosa Island. The point is 2.8 inches long.

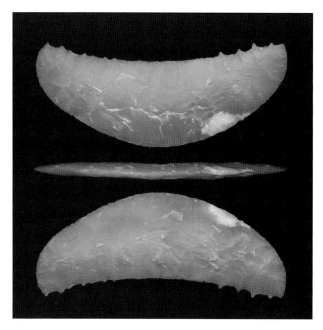

Figure 2.6. A large chipped stone crescent, 3.6 inches long, from San Miguel Island.

islanders also foraged in an ancient estuary near the east end of present-day Santa Rosa Island. Other sites found in high overlook locations with commanding views have produced crescents and stemmed points but no organic remains for radiocarbon dating. Considering that the coastal lowlands of the time have all now been submerged or lost to erosion, and large parts of the islands have yet to be searched, the number of Late Pleistocene sites found in recent years suggests that Paleocoastal people were more numerous on the northern Channel Islands than either of us would have imagined a few years ago. Did those people have a deeper history of island occupation and population growth that remains to be discovered? Only further research will answer that question.

For now, what does this all mean for the first Californians and the kelp highway hypothesis? That Paleoindians lived on the Channel Islands challenges archaeologists to consider new models for the peopling of the Americas, the antiquity of California's maritime people, and the development of the state's remarkable coastal cultures. Were these early islanders descended from Clovis hunters? A decade ago we would have guessed that they were. Today we know people were on the northern Channel Islands during Clovis times, but no Clovis-style spear points have ever been found on the islands. Instead, the stemmed points and crescents from Paleocoastal island sites hint at links to broader cultural developments in western North America and around the Pacific Rim. Similar points and crescents are common at early sites in the American Far West—for instance, at sites clustered around the ancient lakes and marshes of the Great Basin. Recent research suggests that this "Western Stemmed Tradition," once believed to be derived from Clovis, is as old as or older than Clovis. It probably developed independently from Clovis, and it may be derived from a coastal migration from northeast Asia into the Americas. At Paisley Caves, adjacent to an ancient lake in central Oregon, interdisciplinary work led by the University of Oregon's Dennis Jenkins has shown that Paleoindian people used the caves 14,300 years ago, at least a millennium before Clovis technology appeared in North America.

Did these early Americans move westward from the continental interior, or did they spread eastward following Pacific coast rivers into the Great Basin? We do not know for sure, but support for the coastal route comes from recent studies of human DNA and the distribution of similar stemmed points in Late

Figure 2.7. Torben Rick excavating a deeply buried, 11,750-year-old Paleocoastal layer at CA-SRI-512 on Santa Rosa Island.

Pleistocene sites around the Pacific Rim, from Japan and Kamchatka to Oregon, the Channel Islands, and South America. Much remains to be learned about the first Californians, but what is clear is that the California coast is now crucial to understanding the peopling of the Americas and the early ecological history of humans in the New World.

Figure 3.1. Black abalones compete for space on intertidal rocks on the coast of Santa Rosa Island in 1983.

Paradise Found...and Lost...on the Changing California Coast

Patricia Masters and Judith F. Porcasi

Hunkering on overturned plastic buckets, archaeologists sort through finds from a pit dug ten feet into the sandy soil of San Clemente Island. Painstakingly, they separate into labeled plastic bags the bones of long-dead sea lions and dolphins, marine birds, and fish, along with oddly but purposefully shaped chipped rocks. A tribe of blubbery sea lions bickers over basking space on a narrow strip of beach just around the curve of the shore, barking and bellowing a serenade. Suddenly, the air trembles with the report of large artillery. The US Navy is exercising its high-tech muscle in the test battery on the southern tip of the island.

This is the Eel Point archaeological site, in the southern archipelago of the Channel Islands, about sixty miles west of San Diego. Nearly nine thousand years ago people hunted massive marine mammals and fished directly off this promontory of Miocene rock jutting into the Pacific. But this is the Eel Point of today, not that of prehistory. For thousands of years, rising seas and a host of geological and environmental pressures have resculpted the California coastline and offshore islands. Pre-Columbian islanders could have hunted and fished directly off rocky Eel Ridge where it plunged into a deep undersea canyon thrusting far into the Pacific. Dolphins and fish congregated in this virtual underwater highway, bringing a rich marine harvest practically to the islanders' doorstep. Back then the head of the underwater canyon lay only about one hundred feet below the sea surface and the rocky point. Today, it is about two hundred feet under water, and much of the ancient hunting and fishing site is drowned.

Remaining steadfast, Eel Ridge resists these forces. Taking a break from their work, the archaeologists stretch their legs by walking its rock-strewn surface as they consider the loss of the past under water. This has been the fate of much of the California coast. Still, researchers know a great deal about how climate, sea level rise, and shore processes have shaped and continue to reshape the southern California coast—and about how those alterations affected the earliest Californians to live there. We begin our story of the changing coastline thirteen thousand years ago. The Pleistocene geological epoch was drawing to a close after nearly three million years of cycling between glacial climate and warmer intervals. The last ice age glaciation had peaked eighteen thousand years earlier, and the ice caps were melting, yet sea level still stood about 240 feet below its present height.

Imagine, at that time, accompanying the first people to step ashore on Santarosae Island. This super-island encompassed the four northern Channel Islands we know today, as well as some surrounding continental shelf, and one could walk from western-most San Miguel to the eastern tip of Anacapa Island. Covering nearly 350,000 acres, Santarosae sprawled across an area more than two and a half times larger than the four modern islands combined. Larger size meant greater terrestrial resources for the first settlers. The late Pleistocene climate, cooler and wetter than that of today, nurtured pine and cypress forests where remnant herds of pygmy mammoths still roamed. The island's 164 miles of shoreline created habitat for mollusks, marine mammal haul-outs, seabird

Figure 3.2. Bathymetry of the Southern California Bight with extent of exposed shelf and coalesced northern islands at 13,000 (light gray), 10,000 (medium gray), and 9,000 (dark gray) years before present. Note the broad coastal plains on the Santa Barbara, Santa Monica, San Pedro, and San Diego shelves and giant, ancient San Nicolas Island. Elevations range from highest mountains in white to greatest underwater depths in black. The modern coast is the landward side of the dark gray area.

rookeries, kelp forests, and nearshore fisheries —all nourished by the cold, nutrient-rich waters of the California Current flowing south from the Aleutians. Paradise found!

We can experience a bit of that thrill of discovery even today when visiting San Miguel Island. Hiking from the northern landing to the island's ridge, we first become aware of a distant roar. The sound resolves into bellows from thirty thousand seals and sea lions basking and jostling on the western shore at Point Bennett. Further offshore, dolphins and porpoises arc out of the water, and gray whales, orcas, and blue whales spout. In spring and summer, gulls, cormorants, pelicans, and auklets chase across the sky. Oystercatchers join other shorebirds along the beach. Rocky shores and kelp beds teem with sea urchins, abalones, limpets, and mussels. The astounding abundance of marine foods at Santarosae sustained the earliest settlers thirteen thousand years ago and for millennia afterward as human populations expanded along the Santa Barbara coast.

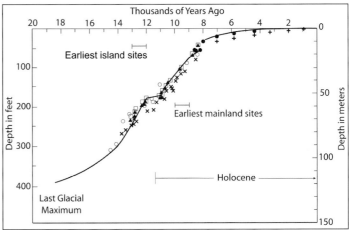

Figure 3.3. Sea level over the past twenty thousand years, drawing on data from six studies in the Pacific Ocean, on the East Coast of the United States, and in the Caribbean Sea.

Vast coastal plains, still exposed at the thirteen-thousand-year sea level, were theirs to explore as well. Between present-day Goleta and Mugu Canyon stretched a territory of more than two hundred thousand acres. Similar broad shelves spanned

Figure 3.4. California sea lions explore a rocky reef at Santa Barbara Island, thirty-eight miles off the coast of southern California and part of the Channel Islands National Marine Sanctuary and Channel Islands National Park.

larder for early fishers and hunters. The early seafarers also made use of the canyon heads to launch their ocean-going craft, because deep water within the canyons prevented waves from breaking and allowed safer passage through the surf zone.

The Dume, Scripps, Eel Point, and Catalina submarine canyons open near headlands or high bluffs. These cliff tops, unlike floodplains and other low-lying areas, are subject to relatively little erosion and tend to preserve archaeological remains. On the wind-swept cliffs at La Jolla and Eel Point, some of the earliest sea mammal hunting sites in North America date to nine thousand years ago and more. The bones of seals, sea lions, and dolphins, as well as those of open ocean fish such as tuna and barracuda, demonstrate the impressive maritime skills of these hunters and fishers at the beginning of the present geological epoch, the Holocene. We see this strategy of hunting sea mammals and fishing off submarine canyons again at seventy-five hundred years ago, judging from dated archaeological finds from Little Harbor on Santa Catalina Island.

the Santa Monica and San Pedro embayments and reached southward from San Diego Bay. Altogether, more than one million acres of exposed coastal plain extended seaward from the present-day coastline. Braided stream valleys cut across these plains, bringing freshwater and riverbank habitat interspersed with grasslands to support mammoths, mastodons, ground sloths, bison, camels, horses, pronghorn, elk, deer, bears, saber-toothed cats, cougars, dire wolves, and coyotes.

Separating these coastal plains, seven steep-walled canyons incise the mainland's shelf and then plunge into the abyss. Three more canyons cut across the shelves of the islands—at Eel Point on San Clemente Island, at the ancient saddle between Santa Rosa and Santa Cruz Islands, and near Little Harbor on the west coast of Santa Catalina Island. Submarine canyons are features of uplifted coasts and follow cracks in the underlying geological formations. Between ten thousand and nine thousand years ago, at a sea level roughly one hundred feet below today's, the canyon heads opened near the shore, bringing cold, nutrient-rich water to the coast. Nutrient upwelling attracts fish and sea mammals while supporting a diversity of nearshore and intertidal invertebrates—another

By nine thousand years ago, the sea had risen to eighty feet below its present level, shrinking Santarosae and separating Anacapa and Santa Cruz Islands from the western landmass. Overall, the sea had claimed seven hundred thousand acres of coastal plain from the islands and the mainland. Dozens of small estuaries formed along the rocky western Santa Barbara coast as the rising sea invaded its many steep stream valleys. These habitats served up abundant clams, oysters, and scallops for early people until around seven thousand years ago, when stream-borne sediment choked the estuaries.

This sequence—tidally flushed estuaries giving way to infilled coastal valleys and eventually to sandy

Figure 3.5. Rocky shore at La Jolla, California, studded with California mussels. Rocky coasts and sandy coasts contrast sharply in food resources.

beaches seven thousand to five thousand years ago— became the evolutionary theme of the remainder of the Holocene on the southern California coast. When sea level was lower during the ice age, streams crossing the exposed shelves cut deep-sided valleys. With sea level rise, marine waters invaded these valleys, creating estuaries. When the rate of sea level rise slowed around six thousand years ago, sediment eroded from the watersheds began to accumulate at the heads of the estuaries. Once the estuaries filled with sediment, floods could carry sand to the outer coast, creating deltas. Currents transported this sand downcoast, forming beaches that blanketed the rocky shore. As long as streams supplied sand to the coast in excess of the amount lost to deeper water and submarine canyons, sandy beaches continued to build. This transition from rocky to sandy coast was completed on the mainland of southern California around five thousand years ago and coincided with the stabilization of sea level near its present-day height. Today, only rocky headlands and tide pools remain to give us a glimpse of the ancient rocky coast and its riches.

Today, Californians enjoy the beauty and recreational value of sand beaches, but sandy coasts had a significant downside for mid-Holocene maritime hunters, fishers, and collectors. Judging by numbers of edible fish, bird, and invertebrate species and their abundance, the subsistence value of sand beaches ranks well below that of rocky coasts and estuaries. When sand blanketed the coast during the mid-Holocene, the net decline in biodiversity and biomass affected all coastal food webs—shellfish, fish, birds, and marine mammals. In turn, the decline created challenges for prehistoric people trying to make a living on the coast. Paradise lost.

Or was it lost? The weather pattern known as El Niño opened another chapter in the story of California's changing environment. El Niño conditions are created when a pool of warmer-than-average water builds in the east-central tropical Pacific. The opposite condition, known as La Niña, is characterized by cooler-than-normal water temperatures in the tropical Pacific. El Niño, along with associated atmospheric changes, is the major cause of annual to decadal

Figure 3.6. Sandy beaches attract visitors and protect the coast from storm waves but provide few food resources.

variations in climate worldwide, and the coast of California is especially sensitive to its phases. During La Niña years, winter storm fronts moving south from the Aleutian Islands bring rain to Washington and Oregon, while southern California receives little rainfall. During El Niño winters, storms come instead from the west, and heavy rains strike California. El Niños generate greater streamflow, higher waves, and coastal erosion. They also disrupt coastal ecosystems.

Although some El Niños occurred early in the Holocene, the period from ten thousand to five thousand years ago saw relatively few El Niños, and southern California experienced a long, mild, dry period. Then, around five thousand years ago, El Niño events abruptly increased. On the Santa Barbara coast, floods may have reopened the estuaries, but in the far south, greater sediment yield from San Diego's semi-arid watersheds caused lagoons to fill with sediment, and their food resources diminished. Higher surface temperatures in nearshore waters throughout southern California drove cold, nutrient-rich water to greater

depths, forcing fish into deeper water and starving seabirds and marine mammals. Warmer ocean temperatures disrupted kelp forests and the nearshore food web as well. Nesting failures and abandoned rookeries marked the frequent El Niños. Meanwhile, inland valleys and foothills flourished with the increased rainfall, which led to growing stocks of birds and mammals for hunting. All these factors may have influenced a shift in human settlement patterns from the coast to the interior that apparently took place along the San Diego and Newport coasts after three thousand years ago.

The last thousand years have seen even greater climatic instability. Some centuries witnessed thirty or more El Niño events, and at other times droughts lasted two hundred years. Despite the fluctuating climate, California's pre-Columbian people diversified and thrived—finding ways to innovate, trade, and create families, art, ritual, and complex social networks in many island and mainland environments. One paradise lost, others found.

Figure 4.1. Controlled burning of an experimental plot at Pinnacles National Park, California, on December 8, 2011. The burning marked a revival of land management by fire by the Amah Mutsun Tribal Band.

Managing the Land with Fire

Kent G. Lightfoot, Rob Q. Cuthrell, Chuck J. Striplen,
and Mark G. Hylkema

December 8, 2011, will be remembered as a historic day for the Amah Mutsun Tribal Band. After prayers and blessings, a tribal elder knelt to light a fire in the picturesque Pinnacles parkland in central California. Smoke soon billowed from a lively blaze. Quickly, it spread across a patch of mature deergrass plants carpeting a small valley dotted with majestic valley oaks. Joining the noise from the crackling fire were the voices of tribal members who intoned their traditional songs to the beat of clapper sticks.

It was a day of celebration—for the first time in more than a century, the Amah Mutsun were intentionally burning a portion of their ancestral land to enhance the health and growth of native resources, in this case, the deergrass whose stalks weavers use to make baskets. In collaboration with the staff at Pinnacles National Park (it received national park status in 2013) and with the able assistance of federal fire specialists, tribal members participated in the controlled burn of a two-acre experimental plot in the park. Over the next few years, a cadre of indigenous scholars, environmental scientists, archaeologists, and resource managers would examine the effects of the fire on the deergrass plants, analyze soil nutrients and microscopic plant remains, make observations about plant and animal diversity, and search for archaeological remains inside and outside the blackened plot. The burn rejuvenated the deergrass plants by removing dead foliage and enhancing the growth of new stems.

The experiment at Pinnacles was part of a renaissance taking place in California in which researchers explore the way Native people's methods for managing their landscapes shaped local ecosystems across the state. Scholars increasingly recognize that Indians used a great variety of methods to enhance the quantity and diversity of plant and animal communities on which they depended for food, medicine, and raw materials for crafts and ceremonial regalia. California Indians actively managed local landscapes by pruning stems and coppicing shrubs and trees (cutting them close to the ground), by removing undergrowth and debris from stands of nut-producing trees, by tilling and weeding demarcated plots of wild plants, and, in a few places, even by digging irrigation canals. At the scale of the broad landscape, intentional burning was their most effective tool for enhancing the vigor and health of plant and animal communities.

California is an ideal place to practice land management by fire. Its Mediterranean climate makes for predictable seasons—wet winters that support dense plant growth, and dry, often hot summers that suck the moisture from duff, grasses, and downed timber, all excellent fuels for fires. Because California in recent years has suffered catastrophic firestorms that destroyed human lives and homes, most Californians today fear wildland conflagrations. But indigenous peoples learned to live with and make constructive use of landscape fires over countless generations. Although burns can be destructive, they can also be highly beneficial to indigenous ecosystems and the people who depend on them for a living. Human-induced, or "anthropogenic," burning can serve many purposes. For example, people may use fire to clear the undergrowth from woodlands for pathways and

Figure 4.2. Charred deergrass plants after the burn at Pinnacles National Park. The plants showed vibrant growth the following year.

harvesting areas. With fire they can transform shrublands, many of which produce few edible seeds or fruits, into productive, seed-bearing grasslands and meadows. They can make game hunting easier, control insect and pest infestations, and encourage plants to produce young, straight stems useful for fashioning cordage, baskets, and other household materials.

We believe California Indians augmented the biological diversity and distinctive microclimates and habitats of their territories by strategically using fire. Small fires set in rotational sequence over a number of years within a tribe's territory would have created mosaics of vegetation at different stages of plant succession. In the years following a fire, different combinations of plants, insects, and animals colonize and flourish in burned areas. Herbaceous plants such as wildflowers and grasses typically take root early in the successional cycle, to be gradually replaced by shrubs and trees over time. By creating patchworks of unevenly aged habitats across their territories, California Indians maintained a reliable assortment of nuts, seeds, fruits, greens, and bulbs even in relatively lean years. The patchy distribution of habitats also supported large numbers of animals and facilitated game hunting.

The current image of California Indians as active managers of the landscape is a far cry from the way early anthropologists depicted them, as passive hunter-gatherers who foraged for wild foods across relatively pristine terrain. Indeed, previous generations of scholars viewed California as something of an enigma. Native California boasted the highest human population densities and greatest linguistic diversity north of Mexico, and most of its peoples lived in semi-permanent villages with complex social and political organizations. Yet the economies of its indigenous peoples, except in a few areas in the southern part of the state, were not based on traditional agriculture—that is, on growing genetically altered, domesticated plants that depended on humans for their reproduction (typically corn, beans, and squash in North America). In classifying California Indians as hunter-gatherers whose livelihoods depended on harvesting wild plants and animals, anthropologists had trouble explaining why they differed so much from many other hunter-gatherers, who were highly mobile peoples living in small, widely scattered bands with little political complexity.

We now recognize that California Indians employed sophisticated cultivation methods to promote the numbers and predictability of a profusion of plants and animals across their territories. These landscape management practices, unlike those of indigenous farmers, did not depend on a few genetically modified crops grown in well-demarcated fields. Rather, California Indians flexibly tended a range of grasses, greens, bulbs, fruits, nuts, and game that grew naturally in their tribal lands. Depending on local climate and the timing of the last fire, people might harvest different mixes of plants and animals in local habitats from one year to the next. By implementing a rotational sequence of small fires across the area and monitoring the growth of plants after each fire, local tribes were able to maintain sustainable economies over many centuries.

There is much that we do not yet know about landscape management by California Indians. Our current understanding draws primarily on observations penned by explorers and settlers in the late 1700s and early 1800s, on a few descriptions written by anthropologists in the early 1900s, after state and federal fire cessation policies were enacted, and on tribal narratives. Often these sources are short on details. The best sources are Native narratives—oral traditions of management practices handed down over several generations—although the contents of these stories vary according to the kinds of colonial entanglements a group experienced. For example, few tribal groups in central and southern California,

who confronted Franciscan missionaries and Russian fur hunters more than two centuries ago, have many recollections about the use of fire because colonial authorities prohibited them from burning the countryside as early as 1793. Northerly tribes, in contrast, were able retain their burning practices in one form or another until relatively recently. In many places, colonizers and settlers actually tried to mimic Native burning practices to maintain open prairies for hunting and farming.

As a result of all this, pinning down precisely when and what kinds of fire traditions were ended, replaced by others, or continued until later years can be challenging. Only recently have archaeologists begun to explore evidence for indigenous land management practices in California, primarily because of the difficulty of differentiating natural fires from human-ignited burns. Telling one kind of fire from the other is especially hard in places where indigenous burning mimicked natural fire regimes, producing subtle shifts in relative densities of indigenous plants and animals. Still, new kinds of eco-archaeological programs are using state-of-the-art methods for documenting past fire regimes, vegetation transformations, and human modifications of the landscape.

Our team is researching indigenous landscape management mainly around the Quiroste Valley Cultural Preserve near Point Año Nuevo, north of Monterey Bay. The Quiroste Valley, situated about a mile inland from the coast, makes a satisfying place for Native people to live. Low hills protect the valley from coastal winds, and a small stream flows through it year-round. Along the stream banks grow lush woodlands of alder, buckeye, and redwood trees. Before twentieth-century farmers drained the valley, it held a marsh with tule reeds that Native people used to make boats, thatch buildings, and clothes. They also dried and ground the tule roots for flour. From the Quiroste Valley, people could easily reach coastal resources such as mollusks, fish, sea mammals, olive shells, and black Monterey chert, as well as plants that grew most abundantly on the slopes and ridges of the Coast Ranges, such as acorns, manzanita berries, and huckleberries.

We carefully selected this location for our fire management study for several reasons. Foremost was the infrequency of lightning fires on this part of the

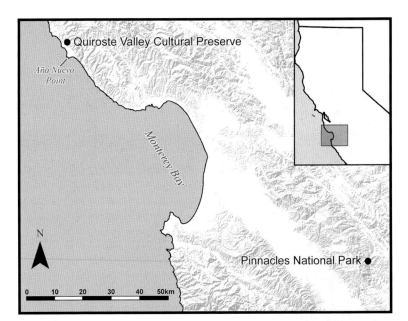

Figure 4.3. Locations of the Quiroste Valley Cultural Preserve and Pinnacles National Park along the central California coast.

Figure 4.4. A view of the Quiroste Valley Cultural Preserve during fieldwork. Note the shrubland and woodland vegetation encroaching into the valley.

Figure 4.5. Archaeological excavations in the Quiroste Valley with members of the Amah Mutsun Tribal Band.

California coast. Fire researchers have estimated that lightning-ignited fires swept through this area in the past only about once or twice a century. Under those conditions, the landscape would have been covered in shrublands and forests most of the time, with grasslands restricted to places where woody plants could not grow. Frequent burning by Natives, in contrast, would likely have suppressed woody vegetation and encouraged grasslands to expand. We also chose this area because it contains vast public lands for ecological sampling, archaeological sites from different time periods, and a documented history of landscape use since the mid-1800s.

Archaeological sites in the Quiroste Valley tell us that it was home to Native people for thousands of years. In the archaeological part of our work, we excavated at a place where Quiroste Indians and their ancestors lived from about a thousand years ago to the beginning of Spanish colonization in the late 1700s. We think this place is the site of a settlement

described in 1769 by members of the first Spanish land expedition, who wrote that it held about two hundred people and a large ceremonial building.

During excavations, we used a technique called flotation, in which we immersed archaeological sediments in specially constructed water tanks to separate charred plant remains, which float to the surface, from soil and other materials, which sink. The plant remains showed that grassland seeds such as those from perennial bunchgrasses, tarweed, and clover were important foods for people who lived in the Quiroste Valley from about 1000 to 1300 CE. We think that without frequent burning by Native people, the extent of grasslands around the valley would have been small, and people would have had to rely more on other plants for food. We also found larger than expected numbers of hazelnut shells among the charred plant remains. Apparently, people regularly ate these nuts, which today are produced only sporadically in wild stands. Early Spanish explorers described

Figure 4.6. Hazelnut shells recovered from the flotation of archaeological deposits in the Quiroste Valley.

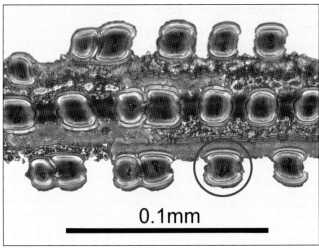

0.1mm

Figure 4.7. Interlocking phytoliths from stems of deergrass, showing distinctive saddle-shaped cells (one is circled at bottom right).

how Indians in this region managed hazel thickets through burning. Possibly the burning invigorated the hazel plants to produce more nuts and to send up more shoots, which could be used for basketry.

Our team also used several ecological techniques to reconstruct the history of vegetation and fire in the area. One of the oldest and best established methods for this type of research is the analysis of pollen and microscopic charcoal from wetland sediment cores—samples of mud carefully extracted from the bottoms of ponds. We collected cores from two ponds near the Quiroste Valley. The first core, from a small pond in the midst of a redwood forest above the valley, suggested that little burning had taken place in the forest understory over the last three thousand years. The second core, from a much older marsh near the coast, indicated regular burning over at least the past five thousand years and possibly much longer, judging from changes in the kinds of plant pollen it contained and from its increasing accumulation of charcoal from local fires. Together the cores revealed that fires became increasingly frequent on the central California coast during the last several thousand years.

Another way in which we are reconstructing the history of vegetation and fire in our study area is by studying cross sections of trees—the stumps of previously logged redwoods—for evidence of fire scars in tree rings caused by burning. This technique lets us

identify the precise years in which landscapes burned and the extent of landscape fires going back a thousand years or more. So far, redwood fire scars have told us that fires were relatively frequent in the last four hundred years or so, with a median "fire return interval" of just four years. We also found a strong relationship between fires and Native village sites, in that we documented more fires closer to historic Native communities.

From soil samples taken in and around the Quiroste Valley, our team also analyzed microscopic structures called silica phytoliths, which form in and around the cells of some types of plants. Grasses and sedges in our research area produce abundant phytoliths, but the local trees rarely form them. With a chemical structure similar to glass, phytoliths can survive in soils for thousands of years. By measuring the quantities of phytoliths in soil samples, we were able to estimate the minimum amount of time during which grasslands must have covered the landscape. We estimated that hundreds of years to more than a thousand years of dense grassland vegetation would have been required to produce the quantities of phytoliths we observed. We think these high levels of phytolith content could not have developed without frequent burning by Native people.

Like the residents of the Quiroste Valley, Indians all up and down the California coast, as well as their inland neighbors, managed their landscapes in sophisticated ways, most notably by intentional burning. Rather than depending on a few genetically modified cultivars grown in confined fields, California Indians enhanced the productivity of a constellation of wild plants and animals in many habitats across their tribal territories for thousands of years. Eco-archaeological studies in California offer exceptional opportunities to better understand these age-old management practices. Local tribes such as the Amah Mutsun Tribal Band, together with resource managers and policy makers, will use the findings of investigations like ours as they apply lessons from the past to the management of their modern landscapes.

Acknowledgments

The funding for our eco-archaeological project has been generously provided by the California Department of Parks and Recreation, the National Science Foundation (BCS-0912162), the Gordon and Betty Moore Foundation, and the Joint Fire Science Program.

Figure 5.1. A Chumash crew landing a plank canoe, or *tomol* in the Chumash language, through heavy surf off the southern California coast, 2008.

Watercraft in Coastal California

Matthew Des Lauriers

The sea glittered beneath us as our eighteen-foot boat slammed its way through each rising swell. Cold spray prickled our cheeks. Behind us receded the rocky, kelp-festooned tip of Punta Eugenia, Baja California, whose ethereally lonely little fishing village we had left half an hour earlier. On our port side we passed the thin shard of an island today called Isla Natividad, with its own fishing village and a famous point break known to modern surfers as "Open Doors." The native Cochimí people of the region named the island Afegua, "island of the birds," for the phenomenal numbers of seabirds that once nested there.

Before us rose our destination, the steep four-thousand-foot peak of Isla Cedros, or Huamalgua, "island of the fogs." Although that day had dawned clear and sunny and we found our way to the island easily, thick ocean mists often hold the flanks of Isla Cedros in their embrace. We had previously made this crossing both at twilight and in storm, but the most gut-wrenching of all was in dense, impenetrable fog.

Here, at the southern end of the Southern California Bight, more than four hundred miles south of the US-Mexico border, heading for our archaeological dig on Isla Cedros, we were sharing an experience that had defined life along the coast of California for thousands of years. We were crossing the paradoxical sea, simultaneously a barrier and a bridge, from one small world to another. Like generations of seafarers before us, we faced a seemingly vast body of water with waves and currents that would challenge the most athletic of swimmers, even without great white sharks on patrol.

Boats, canoes, rafts, watercraft—by whatever name one wishes to use, vessels that floated on water created one of the first great transportation revolutions in human history. Long before the first horse was ridden or the first ox hitched to a cart, humans used boats. Boats took the first people to Australia, and recent research suggests that people first arrived in California by paddling down the coast from their homeland in Beringia, now partly drowned. Their descendants preserved many of the voyagers' traditions and knowledge regarding the sea, its riches, and its dangers.

In their elegantly simple vessels, those descendants—among them the Huamalgüeños of Cedros Island and the Chumash and Tongva peoples of today's southern California—sailed much farther out to sea than the later Spaniards cared to in the rowboats they stowed aboard their ships. All the Channel Islands had to have been settled from the sea. Chumash oral tradition holds that the original eight families on Santa Cruz Island arrived as refugees after fleeing a "civil war" on the mainland. A hundred centuries of history rode on the vessels first described in writing by early Spanish explorers, and they served their makers well. Ultimately, they enabled the survivors of European colonization and diseases, refugees of a different sort, to depart the islands. Those holdouts reluctantly left their island homes in much the same way their ancestors had arrived, aboard watercraft made by their own hands.

Along the coast of California, as elsewhere throughout the Americas, the workhorse of small watercraft was the tule balsa. As its name implies (the word *tule* comes from a Mexican Indian name for bulrushes), people fashioned these boats from rushes, reeds, or both. The makers first bound tightly packed reeds together in bundles and then lashed several bundles together to form the boat, the number of bundles determining its size. Usually the number was either three or five, one of which was a central bundle forming the keel of the craft. The tules' natural buoyancy made the boats resistant to sinking. Considering that many coastal groups produced basketry of exceptional technical quality and artistic skill, perhaps it should be no surprise that they also created "woven" watercraft.

Figure 5.2. Native people in a tule balsa in San Francisco Bay. Using double-bladed paddles, oarsmen could attain significant speed; balsas were not limited to being poled through shallow water. Hand-tinted lithographic reproduction of an 1816 drawing by Louis Choris.

The versatile balsa could be a tiny, one-person vessel, little more than a raft, or a sizable boat fit to carry several people and a fair amount of cargo. Early residents of the San Francisco Bay area, who enjoyed an abundance of reed marshes in the past (plate 24), produced large tule balsas that were well made, seaworthy, and capable of being propelled swiftly through the water with double-bladed paddles. The Seri Indians of northwestern Mexico regularly navigated the tempestuous Gulf of California in balsas. Within the relatively calm Southern California Bight, balsas served nicely for fishing and coastwise trips in all but exceptionally rough seas. Chumash, Tongva, and especially Kumeyaay Indians, like many others along the coast, used tule balsas routinely in estuaries and on lakes and rivers.

Common to the traditions of many Native American groups, the tule balsa is clearly an ancient, foundational form of watercraft. The first Californians might have arrived aboard such boats after a long run down a virgin coastline; at the very least they began to build such craft more than twelve thousand years ago. Some of the first crossings from the California mainland to the Channel Islands likely took place in balsas. Even the outermost Channel Islands, San Nicolas and San Clemente, saw human settlement by eighty-five

hundred years ago, and people doubtless arrived on the nearer islands earlier than that.

Ancient in form and relatively easy to make, balsas held many advantages over heavier, more complex boats: the materials needed to make them cost little, and the craft offer good buoyancy and ease of landing. Even into colonial times, Franciscan missionaries reported seeing Native people make the trip out to Santa Catalina Island aboard tule balsas.

Yet for all its deep antiquity and great usefulness, the tule balsa was not the apogee of Native Californian naval technology. That title must go to the plank canoe, used exclusively by the Chumash and Tongva. In the Chumash language, spoken between today's San Luis Obispo and Ventura Counties, the plank canoe was a *tomol*, and in Tongva, the language of the original inhabitants of the Los Angeles basin and coastline, it was a *ti'at*. Plank canoes are not to be confused with the better-known and very different dugout vessels that Indians of the Northwest Coast developed to such a great degree of mastery. At the time of European contact, dugouts appeared only rarely south of San Francisco Bay, undoubtedly because of the shortage of large, straight-trunked trees along the more southerly coast.

Figure 5.3. A Seri Indian youth with a small tule balsa. The Seri people of the northwestern Mexico coast continue to make and launch these crafts.

planks and drilled holes in them. Running fine cordage through the holes, they sewed the planks together, setting crosspiece seats amidships and toward the bow and stern to spread the sides of the vessel apart. Builders made their craft as waterproof as possible by caulking the seams between the planks with tar collected from natural seeps (plate 17). Still, as one Spanish explorer observed in 1600, the canoes had a tendency to leak and often required one crew member to bail out water continuously.

It may well have been the ready availability of tar in coastal southern California that prompted the invention of the plank canoe there. Driftwood is abundant along many parts of the Pacific coast, but few places are as richly bestowed with natural tar seeps as the coast of southern California. Tar seeps at places like Carpinteria and the world-famous tar pools at La Brea, now on Wilshire Boulevard in downtown Los Angeles, undoubtedly helped shape southern California maritime technology. The labor required to hew, sew, and caulk logs into a seaworthy vessel dwarfed the effort and material costs required to make a tule balsa, and the investment made plank canoes extremely valuable to their owners.

Instead, Native peoples from San Francisco Bay southward took what at first glance seems a poor set of raw materials—driftwood, tar, and cordage twisted from fibers of the milkweed plant—and fashioned them into a beautiful, sleek form of canoe that quickly became indispensable to coastal life and commerce. By hand the canoe makers hewed planks from redwood and cedar logs that had drifted down the coast from as far north as British Columbia. Carefully, they smoothed the margins and ends of the

Exactly when people began building plank canoes is unknown, but it was at least by 500 CE, when Native Californians had colonized even the most distant Channel Islands. Archaeologist Lynn Gamble has convincingly followed traces of the tomol back at least thirteen hundred years, which coincides well with the emergence along the coast of a complex system of trade in foodstuffs and durable goods such as shell beads during the last fifteen hundred years before the arrival of Europeans. This lucrative trade gave Native people good reason to invent a vessel that could carry heavier loads than a tule balsa could handle. The plank canoe became the lynchpin in a transportation system that, on the islands lying off Santa Barbara, spurred the production of shell beads for use as money (chapter 12). On Santa Catalina Island, plank canoe transport underpinned the surprisingly industrial-scale manufacture of steatite stone bowls for widespread trade. Without the high-sided, fast-moving, large-cargo-bearing plank canoe, none of the commerce, craft specialization, chiefly competition, and social hierarchy that characterized the late pre-Columbian tribes along the southern California coast would ever have developed.

These canoes became integrated into every level of Chumash and Tongva culture, from the economic arena to the social and political realms and even to metaphysical beliefs and legends. Economically, for example, people who owned plank canoes—an expensive capital investment—not only profited from trade but also possessed a means to perform favors for others, by transporting them and their goods. Such favors formed a kind of "social capital" that boat owners could draw on to obtain help in times of crisis or to secure favors for allies and family members. Ambitious elites and members of the "brotherhood of the tomol"—a kind of guild that defined who could own a canoe—constructed and deployed their canoes to create and maintain networks of social obligation and political influence.

Figure 5.4. The *Mo'omat Ahiko*, a Tongva *ti'at* (*left*) and the *'Elye'wun*, a Chumash *tomol*, photographed off the coast of Catalina Island in 1998. Both are southern California plank canoes.

Much of what we know about plank canoes comes from notes compiled by the ethnographer John P. Harrington in the early twentieth century, which were edited and published in 1978 as the book *Tomol: Chumash Watercraft as Described in the Ethnographic Notes of John P. Harrington*. Through Harrington, Chumash elders such as Fernando Librado Kitsepawit, one of the last Chumash people to have seen tomols made and used before the end of the nineteenth century, left a permanent record of the way in which the whole of Chumash society—its geography, ecology, technological know-how, social networks, trade, belief systems, and art—intersected in the tomol. "The First Man in this world," Librado told Harrington in 1914, "said that all the world is a canoe."

The stories Librado and others told Harrington, like the tales of seafaring people everywhere, abound with perils of the sea and the bravery of canoe crews. Although sturdy enough for long-distance travel, tomols were scarcely without risk, and Librado recounted many tales of drownings and sinkings of canoes during dangerous channel crossings. One

Figure 5.5. A Chumash *tomol* being constructed in 1912 under the direction of Fernando Librado Kitsepawit (*far right*) for J. P. Harrington. The boat was never taken to sea.

story described a journey made under the direction of a healer and canoe maker named Palatino Saqt'ele. After one of two canoes on the voyage sank, and with his own taking on water, Palatino stood up and shouted three times in a falsetto voice. Suddenly, a falcon, or *helek*, appeared and led the distressed craft to shore, saving the lives of its crew. The first modern tomol ever to be built, under the auspices of the Santa Barbara Museum of Natural History in 1976, was christened *Helek*.

The *Helek* is part of a revival of the ancient plank canoe tradition by a new generation of Native Californians and other indigenous people of the Pacific coast—Chumash and Tongva as well as groups in northwestern Mexico, Washington State, British Columbia, and Alaska. Often they effectively use traditional watercraft as the centerpieces of movements to revitalize Native culture and language. Building and launching such vessels, which embody ancestral ways, bring Native people much closer to their deep heritage than talking and writing about it can ever do (plate 11). For these people, the experience of *being* between two worlds—between the land and the sea, between the past and the present—must be lived in order to be understood, and the revival of their ancestors' watercraft makes that experience possible.

Figure 6.1. Archaeologist Nels Nelson taking a break during excavation work at the Emeryville shell mound, 1906.

Shell Mound Builders of San Francisco Bay

Kent G. Lightfoot, Edward M. Luby, Matthew A. Russell,
and Tsim D. Schneider

Animated voices called from the top of a huge shell mound rising above the shore of San Francisco Bay. The time was five centuries ago, and people were making their way from their cone-shaped, tule-reed homes, perched on the mound twenty feet above the bay, down a path along the side of the artificial hill. At the bottom, some women and men headed out in reed boats to fish the bay for surfperches and jacksmelts. A party of young men, camouflaged in ochre body paint and animal skins, turned toward the hills to hunt deer and elk in the oak woodlands. A noisy group of men and women tramped down to a place on the shoreline known for its prolific clam and oyster beds. With baskets, digging tools, and children in tow, they collected shellfish to carry back to their village for an upcoming funeral feast.

Other residents stayed behind to prepare for the gathering, which would be hosted at the mound village to commemorate the passing of a young woman who would be buried that night near her family's house. Several women cleaned out a large underground oven in which to cook shellfish and venison for the main meal. Removing from the oven the fire-cracked rocks, discarded shells, and broken animal bones from the previous night's meal, they dumped the debris in a part of the mound where no one currently lived. Nearby, a woman steadily ground grass seeds and acorns. Later, she would place the seed-and-nut meal in a watertight basket, mix it with water, and boil it into a gruel by stirring small, heated rocks into the basket. She would discard the rocks, along with the ash and charcoal from the hearth, in the same place as the detritus from the underground oven. In these ways, villagers continued to raise the height of their human-made hill one meal at a time.

Five men stayed to dig a deep grave for the deceased woman behind her family's house. Her family and neighbors would bury her lying on her left side with her legs drawn up and her head resting on her folded hands. They would place in the grave with her a few items she had cherished in life—a pestle, a bone awl, and her shell bead necklace. Earlier, the men had gone to considerable effort to obtain three baskets of clean sand and pebbles, a handful of red ochre, and two large rocks, which they carried to the top of the mound. When they buried their kinswoman that evening, they would help dedicate the burial place to her by adding the ochre, sand, and stones to the grave, together with shells and animal bones from the mortuary feast, representing the staff of life on the bay. Burials, too, helped build up the mound over time.

One young man rested briefly from digging the burial pit with a fire-hardened digging stick. Despite the sadness of the day, he enjoyed the spectacular waterfront view and looked forward to seeing relatives and friends from surrounding communities at the ceremony and feast that night. The weather promised to hold clear, affording a view across the bay at the twinkling campfire lights of scores of other mound villages on the other side. His people's mounds, he thought, were like nothing else in the landscape— they were places of family, food, and ancestors. They were home.

Figure 6.2. Nels Nelson's excavation trench at the Ellis Landing Shellmound, 1906.

Skip ahead four hundred years since that star-filled night, to the year 1906. The great mound, now abandoned by Native people, has become the site of a quarrying operation producing garden soil and road fill for the new cities of San Francisco, Berkeley, and nearby Richmond. Nels Nelson and A. W. Wepfer, archaeologists from the University of California, are conducting scientific excavations at the untouched center of the shell mound, aiming to collect a sample of materials before the mound is totally destroyed. They dig a trench six feet wide and nearly a hundred feet long, reaching from the mound's center to its edge along the marshlands. Carefully, the two men record the locations of stone tools, bone artifacts, shell ornaments, animal bones, ash deposits, rock clusters, and other significant remains.

Wiping dirt from his eyeglasses, Nelson scribbles in his dog-eared Blue Bond field journal his observations about the site for July 19, 1906. The mound, he notes, measures about 460 feet long and 246 feet

wide. He and Wepfer have named it the Ellis Landing Shellmound. They are fascinated by the dense concentration of rocks, pebbles, sand deposits, ash concentrations, shell detritus, and burned bone that make up the mound's complex sequence of layers. They are also intrigued by the large number of Indians who were buried in the mound. Extrapolating from the findings in their trench, they calculate that at least three thousand bodies and possibly as many as ten thousand were entombed there over the years.

Fast forward now to 2014. Shockingly, nearly all of the multitude of shell mounds that once ringed the shores of San Francisco Bay have been flattened. Some have been cleared to make way for farming; others have been mined for garden soil, fertilizer, and material for roadways and tennis courts. Ultimately, most have fallen victim to the rapid urban development of the bay shore.

Fortunately, more than a century ago archaeologists like Nels Nelson described more than 425

Figure 6.3. The Greenbrae shell mound, another archaeological site dug by Nels Nelson in the greater San Francisco Bay area, in 1909. An excavation trench cuts through the center of the mound.

Figure 6.4. Museum-based research in action: a shell artifact from the Ellis Landing site receives analysis.

mounds in considerable detail and took photographs of them before they were destroyed. These pioneering scholars also excavated some of the largest shell mounds, such as the Ellis Landing, Emeryville, and Greenbrae mounds. Sometimes they did so truly in the nick of time. Nelson was still conducting salvage excavations at Ellis Landing in 1908 as horse-drawn graders removed what was left of the mound.

Today, museums such as the Phoebe A. Hearst Museum of Anthropology (PAHMA) at the University of California, Berkeley, house collections from these early excavations—irreplaceable time capsules for researchers and Native communities. With the destruction of most of the large mounds, archaeologists now rely largely on these collections for research purposes. Small mounds and remnants of larger ones still dot the area in places hidden from the public, such as under parking lots and in protected parklands, but park managers see them as endangered resources, and to local tribes they are sacred places. Because managers hold the principled goal of preserving sites, archaeologists nowadays begin new excavations rarely and with extreme care, usually only at sites that are endangered by the construction of new roads, shopping malls, and houses.

With large-scale archaeological excavations at mounds no longer feasible, it is hard to overestimate the value of early shell mound collections in museums.

For decades museums have curated well-preserved artifacts, animal bones, and soil and shell samples, together with the early archaeologists' excellent field notes, photographs, maps, and illustrations. Researchers are increasingly realizing that these collections can be restudied with new techniques. A renaissance in shell mound research is under way.

We now know that over the last five thousand years, Native groups around San Francisco Bay created a landscape dominated by artificial hills covering areas the size of one or two football fields and rising as much as thirty feet above the ground surface. Slowly, they piled up tons of materials, which archaeologists see as intricate lenses of discarded shells; pockets of soil, ashes, pebbles, and fire-cracked rocks; scattered animal bones; and artifacts of stone, bone, and antler. The largest mounds were central nodes in clusters of medium-sized and small shell mounds, typically situated where freshwater streams emptied into the bay. Beyond the mounds lay an assortment of work spaces and ceremonial areas whose traces today include scatters of stone tools and chipping debris, mortars ground into bedrock that were used for processing nut crops, and rock faces where people once pecked out petroglyphs in abstract designs.

Two recent technologies provide fresh insights into the ages of shell mounds and the ways in which they were built up and used over time. One is the use of computer software called geographical information systems (GIS), a powerful suite of tools with which archaeologists can analyze the precise positions of materials in shell mounds in three-dimensional space. GIS enables researchers to identify clusters of artifacts, food remains, burials, and house structures, from which they can reconstruct the spatial organization of residential areas, work places, and ceremonial spaces in ancient villages.

The other technology is accelerator mass spectrometry (AMS), a way of radiocarbon-dating tiny specimens of organic material. The earliest mound materials that have been dated through AMS in the Bay Area were deposited some five thousand to four thousand years ago, just when sea level rise after the last ice age began to slow enough to create the shoreline of San Francisco Bay as we know it today. Dated charcoal and shell samples taken from the twenty-nine-foot-high trench wall that Nelson exposed in the Ellis Landing mound show that people used the mound episodically for almost thirty-five hundred years, from about 1800 BCE to 1700 CE or later. A similar study involved museum specimens from the Brooks Island site, a smaller shell mound near Ellis Landing excavated in the 1960s by George Coles, whose field notes and collections are curated in the Richmond Museum of History. AMS dates for samples from the Brooks Island mound reveal that people used the site from 850 CE to at least 1720 CE.

The discovery that some mounds saw use into the historic period is especially tantalizing because Native populations changed so dramatically between the beginning of Spanish exploration in 1542 and the end of the colonial period in the 1830s (chapters 14 and 15). The historical record keeps decidedly quiet about whether or not people continued to live on shell mounds after Europeans entered San Francisco Bay. A recent study of mounds in China Camp State Park, on the Marin County bay shore, has shed new light on this question. Nelson visited and recorded the Thomas

Figure 6.5. Charred fragment of a basket excavated from the Thomas site by Clement Meighan in 1949, now curated at the Phoebe A. Hearst Museum of Anthropology. The fragment measures about 1 by 1.6 inches.

mound, now in the park, in the early 1900s. Rising more than thirty feet high, the Thomas mound is the largest of several in a mound cluster. Clement Meighan supervised excavations there in 1949, wrote a report, and curated the archaeological materials at PAHMA.

A recent study of the Thomas site collections, together with a carefully designed, low-impact field investigation of other sites in the mound cluster by scholars from the Federated Indians of the Graton Rancheria and the University of California, Berkeley, has generated a new suite of radiocarbon dates. Two samples of charred basketry collected in 1949 from one of the Thomas site "house pits"—depressions that served as the foundations for conical houses—gave AMS dates ranging between 1630 and 1730. Four dates from another mound in the cluster, including two dates from the bottom of an underground oven, span the centuries from 770 CE to 1810, signaling occupation into the colonial period. Perhaps Indians who resisted moving to the Spanish missions continued to live on the mounds for a while, or perhaps baptized Indians who fled the missions by stealth found refuge there in the secluded hinterlands (chapter 15).

The radiocarbon dates now available reveal that people's uses of shell mounds and the ways in which mounds accumulated changed over time. For example, throughout nearly the first twenty-seven hundred years of its existence, the large Ellis Landing mound served primarily as a place for burials and ceremonies—a place where people periodically gathered for dances, commemorations, feasts, and funeral rites. The mound rose mainly because of the burial of more and more people and the piling up of debris from the accompanying feasts and rituals. Like Ellis Landing, all the largest mounds dug by early archaeologists contained large numbers of human burials—men, women, and children—either in small, demarcated cemeteries or separately as couples and individuals throughout the mound.

After 900 CE the Ellis Landing mound became a vibrant village like the one we imagined at the beginning of this chapter. With many generations of ancestors entombed deep beneath them, people now lived on the artificial hill in houses they built from clay, wood, and tule reeds. Nelson described fifteen house pits on the top of Ellis Landing, and several other possible house floors can be seen in his profile drawing of the upper layers of the site. Excavations at other mounds show that most house floors were circular, measured ten to twenty feet in diameter, and consisted of prepared clay.

In this later period and perhaps continuing into historic times, Ellis Landing served not just as a home for the living and a burial ground for the recently deceased. It was also a place where people memorialized and celebrated their long-ago relatives and the founding members of ancient clans and lineages. As they did so, they feasted on a remarkable range of foods, as we know from analyses of animal remains in museum collections. Residents of the mound villages ate shellfish such as bay mussels, Pacific oysters, and bent-nose clams; terrestrial game such as deer and elk; sea mammals such as sea otters and harbor seals; fish such as bat rays, leopard sharks, surfperch, jacksmelt, sturgeon, and salmon; and birds such as ducks, geese, cormorants, and loons.

Increasingly, state-of-the-art methods for studying such animal remains give researchers new understandings of the shell mounds' environment, the seasons of the year when mounds were inhabited, and even the social relationships between people living in shell mound clusters. For example, measuring the geochemical constituents of shells from ancient shellfish helps us infer water salinity and temperature, which offer clues to the seasons of harvest. A geochemical reading of low salinity usually reflects a winter harvest, because heavier winter rainfall sends more freshwater into San Francisco Bay. A high salinity reading in the shells tends to reflect the opposite—a shellfish harvest during the drier summer.

An analysis of mussel shells from the Ellis Landing and Brooks Island mounds shows that in late pre-Columbian and early historic times, shellfish gatherers were present at both sites throughout most of the year. This discovery is important because it demonstrates that after 900 CE, people lived at both large and small shell mounds contemporaneously, perhaps all as members of a large shell mound community. In another study, seasonality data collected from shellfish samples from a mound in China Camp State Park are being compared with the seasonal movements of Native people to and from local Spanish missions, in order to better understand how shellfishing areas were continuously reused despite the missions' efforts to limit hunting and gathering.

Although most of the shell mounds that once dotted the San Francisco Bay shore have been destroyed, the legacy of Nels Nelson and other early archaeologists lives on in their field collections, now preserved in local museums. These collections continue to fuel research by tribal scholars and archaeologists seeking to understand when, how, and why mounds were piled up across San Francisco's landscape. As researchers develop new technologies and ever more innovative ways of studying museum collections, generations of Native people who once lived on and were buried in the mounds will be commemorated with a greater understanding of their lives.

Acknowledgment

We appreciate greatly the generous support of our shell mound research by the National Science Foundation (BCS-0342658).

Figure 7.1. Archaeological salvage excavations under way in 2009 at a rapidly eroding archaeological site near Diablo Canyon, on the central California coast. Crew members are students and faculty from California Polytechnic State University, San Luis Obispo.

Steinbeck Country before Steinbeck

Terry L. Jones

Standing in line on a blindingly sunny but frigid winter day, waiting for the doors to the Monterey Bay Aquarium to open, I find myself sandwiched between a group of yawning eighth graders on a school trip from California's Central Valley and a young couple speaking intensely in French. Across the parking lot, a bus full of children from nearby Salinas begins to unload, the boys and girls chattering in a mix of Spanish and English. Today, it seems, the spectacular sea life of Monterey Bay, in both its controlled, museum-like state inside and its glorious natural form outside, has drawn a crowd from many twenty- first-century cultural backgrounds.

Few of these visitors are likely to know that the shores of California's central coast—Santa Cruz, Monterey, and San Luis Obispo counties—have been attracting diverse groups for thousands of years. Less than a hundred years ago these were the haunts of John Steinbeck and his pal Doc Ricketts, who teamed up to study and revel in the beauty of the central coast seashore. Ricketts's interest in sea otters, abalones, and rockfish was academic; much of the knowledge conveyed in the aquarium's exhibits of the kelp forests, rocky reefs, and estuaries that dominate this shoreline today is the result of his careful studies. Understanding the lives of the people who visited these shores for millennia before Steinbeck is a different kind of challenge. We know from historical accounts and anthropological descriptions that people with distinctive cultural backgrounds, speaking at least ten languages, lived along the central coast at the time Spaniards first arrived by land, in 1769.

Archaeologists now believe people fished and gathered shellfish on the central coast as early as ten thousand years ago and possibly more than thirteen thousand. Over the centuries, group after group sought the coast's generous resources—often for greatly different reasons.

Accounts written by early European explorers and later anthropologists, in tandem with archaeological discoveries, allow us to piece together a tentative portrait of the central coast's pre-Columbian past. The earliest descriptions of Native Californians were recorded by Spanish seafarers who sailed along the coast in the late 1500s. In 1595, for example, Sebastian Rodríguez Cermeño wrote the following description somewhere near what is now Avila Beach in San Luis Obispo County; it was published in English translation in 1929 in H. R. Wagner's *Spanish Voyages to the Northwest Coast of North America in the Sixteenth Century:*

"There were observed on the shore of the seas many people on top of some bluffs, where they had many settlements. As it was late, I anchored in front of these settlements and I saw how the Indians had on shore many balsas made of tule, which are like reeds…. The balsas were made like canoes, and with these they go fishing. Calling to some of them from the launch…we gave them to understand by signs that they should bring us something to eat, as we had no food. Understanding our necessity, they went ashore and brought some bitter acorns and mush made of these acorns in some dishes made of straw like large chocolate bowls…. They are people well set up, of

Figure 7.2. John Peabody Harrington (*on steps*) with Frank Olivas Jr. and Rosario Cooper (*far right*), the last known speaker of Northern Chumash, in Arroyo Grande, California, 1916.

medium height, of a brown color, and like the rest, go naked, not only the men, but women, although the women wear some skirts made of grass and bird feathers. They use the bow and arrow, and their food consists of bitter acorns and fish. They seemed to be about three hundred in number, counting men, women, and children."

This account establishes some key facts about Native life along the central coast in the 1500s. Unlike the Chumash of the Santa Barbara Channel, these people did not use wooden sewn-plank boats for fishing but rather reed (tule) canoes. Their diet included fish and acorns but no cultivated crops; they used baskets but not pottery; and they hunted with bows and arrows.

Nearly two hundred years later the Portolá expedition, an entourage of sixty-three Spanish soldiers and Indian porters with hundreds of horses and pack animals, traversed the central coast on its way from San Diego to Monterey Bay. Observations by expedition members add details to the portrait of Native life

in central California. On November 19, 1769, near Point Año Nuevo, Fray Juan Crespí—whose chronicle was published in English in Alan K. Brown's *A Description of Distant Roads*—mentioned a village of "very well-behaved, friendly heathens, with a very large grass-roofed house and many other small ones made of upright split sticks. On the way coming up they made us a present of a great many large black pies and many other white-colored ones that appeared to be made from acorns, presenting us also with two pouches of wild leaf tobacco, which I took a fancy to try, and it was not so very poor. Now upon the way returning, everything had been abandoned."

Accounts by Crespí and others suggest that settlements were relatively small, each housing forty to sixty people, and that folk often moved as the seasons changed, leaving one community and erecting new houses in another. In some other parts of California, people resided year-round in the same villages, but worldwide it is not uncommon for hunter-gatherers to migrate in a seasonal cycle.

Figure 7.3. Maria Jesusa Encinales (*right*) and Maria de Los Angeles, two of John P. Harrington's primary Salinan consultants, with another unidentified person in front of an adobe dwelling in southern Monterey County, 1930s.

The early and highly ethnocentric chroniclers failed to recognize the diversity of languages spoken by the groups they met. The array of tongues—and their implications—was not fully appreciated until the late nineteenth and early twentieth centuries, when trained anthropologists began to collect information in central California. These early researchers engaged in "salvage ethnography," trying to record as much as possible about Native lifeways, languages, and traditions before, as white people expected, they were irrevocably lost. Ethnographers sought especially to interview elders who still had some memories of pre-European culture.

By far the most zealous of the salvage anthropologists was John Peabody Harrington, of the Smithsonian Institution, who worked tirelessly between 1902 and 1961 to record Indian languages and culture. His careful studies, along with records compiled at the Spanish missions, document at least ten languages in the Chumashan, Salinan, Esselen, and Costanoan families (see map page x) that were spoken along the central coast. The speakers divided themselves into a multitude of small, fiercely independent groups that the famous California ethnographer Alfred Kroeber called "tribelets." Usually these little tribes each comprised fewer people than those in the large political groups living farther south, along the Santa Barbara Channel, and they had far less hierarchical power structures.

How did peoples speaking a multitude of languages wind up living side by side in small communities with similar lifestyles? Archaeologists have been trying to resolve this question for the last fifty years, but a fully satisfactory answer eludes us. Almost certainly, cultural diversity has a deep history in California. On the central coast we have some faint evidence that big-game hunters visited the region as early as thirteen thousand years ago, arriving from the interior of the continent in pursuit of now-extinct game animals such as mammoths and bison. At nearly the same time, seafood-oriented people seem to have been moving southward into California along the coast by boat. We can only guess at the languages these earliest immigrants spoke, but probably there were more than one.

Our understanding of prehistoric life before ten thousand years ago is little more than conjecture. But beginning around that date, dozens of archaeological sites attest to the appearance on the central coast and in near-coastal valleys of a culture that archaeologists refer to as "Milling Stone." Researchers first recognized it at Diablo Canyon in San Luis Obispo County in the 1960s. Milling Stone people ate a varied diet featuring shellfish, fish, mammals, and birds, with an emphasis on hunting and trapping small animals such as rabbits and ducks rather than large game such as deer and elk.

The defining feature of this culture, though, was a heavy reliance on stone grinding tools. Using large, flat slabs in conjunction with hand-size, flat, square stones that archaeologists cleverly refer to as handstones, people ground small seeds into flour. Such tools show up in tremendous numbers in Milling Stone sites, often outnumbering spear and dart points (bows and arrows still lay far in the future) by a ratio of more than ten to one.

The heavy emphasis on grinding suggested by these tools has led some archaeologists to speculate that men involved themselves more with gathering plant foods during Milling Stone times than they did at the time of European arrival, when California Indian men mostly hunted and fished, and women gathered. Whether the milling tools were used to process acorns, the single most important food throughout Native California at the time of European contact, is uncertain, but the grinding tools associated with acorn processing in historic times—the stone mortar and pestle—are rarely, if ever, found at Milling Stone sites. If Milling Stone people collected acorns, it seems that the nuts were not nearly as important to them as small grass seeds and yucca hearts, the charred remains of which have been collected from the oldest Milling Stone sites.

One curious animal that Milling Stone people pursued along the coast was the flightless sea duck, a goose-size bird that seems to have been related to today's eiders. Like flightless birds worldwide, *Chendytes lawi* was a highly attractive yet vulnerable food source, and excavators have found its bones at many sites in southern and central California. But

Figure 7.4. The Milling Stone culture was first recognized at the base of a deep shell midden near the Diablo Canyon Nuclear Power plant, shown here during excavation in 1968.

none of the flightless duck bones date later than twenty-five hundred years ago, and no one has ever reported seeing the duck in historic times. Apparently, over a span of nearly eight thousand years, coastal Indians hunted the birds to extinction.

For nearly forty-five hundred years, daily life on the central coast found accompaniment in the regular rhythm of women grinding seeds with handstones against milling slabs. Men snared rabbits and birds and once in a great while stalked a deer with hand-held spears or spear-throwers (atlatls). Then, around fifty-five hundred years ago, this lifeway disappeared, to be replaced by a new adaptation heavy on hunting. Hunting equipment in the form of large spear and atlatl dart points, with notches on their sides or with bases narrowed like stems, became abundant even as milling stones grew scarce. Crucially, women began using for the first time the single most important grinding technology of Native California—the mortar and pestle. With their bowl-shaped concavities, mortars are much better suited for grinding large, bulky nuts such as acorns, so it seems that acorns became important from this time onward.

Plate 1. Four Chumash baskets made sometime after European contact and now in the collections of the Santa Barbara Museum of Natural History.

Plate 2. Point Reyes National Seashore, California.

Plate 3. Russell A. Ruiz, *Santa Barbara in 1795 (Forest Fire on Mountains)*, possibly painted in the 1960s. Ruiz interpreted what Santa Barbara might have looked like in 1795, with the Chumash village of Syuxtun in the foreground, the Spanish presidio immediately behind it, and the mission to the left.

Plate 4. The rugged Big Sur shore near Monterey, California, typical of this stretch of coastline.

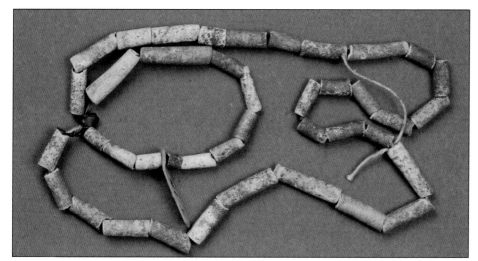

Plate 5. A necklace made of beads stained with red ochre that artisans cut and ground from thick pieces of clamshell. The beads were excavated from archaeological site SCRI-333; the longest ones measure about two-thirds of an inch.

Plate 6. One of two traditional-style ceremonial baskets made by the Rumsien Ohlone basketry artist Linda Yamane between 2009 and 2012 for the Oakland Museum of California. It contains 12,300 stitches, 110 willow sticks, and about 400 sedge weaving strands; its continuous coil measures 60 feet long.

Plate 7. The second of two ceremonial baskets by Linda Yamane, decorated with olive shell beads, red-dyed feathers, and abalone shell pendants. For their maker, baskets like these interweave the earth's energy with the weaver's will to transform everyday materials into vessels of extraordinary beauty.

Plate 8. Oak grove in Santa Barbara, California. Oak trees gave California Indians an important food in the form of acorns, which could be stored for years.

Plate 9. Spectacular, enigmatic Chumash paintings at Pleito Creek, California. Exemplary of Chumash artistic expression, these are among the finest pre-Columbian pictographs in North America.

Plate 10. In a painting by Gordon Miller, local Indians observe the repair of Sir Francis Drake's ship, the *Golden Hind*, in 1579, probably in present-day Marin County, California. The Indians' small boats, or *balsas*, made of tule reeds, are of a style typical of the San Francisco Bay area.

Plate 11. The *'Elye'wun*, a sleek, fast plank canoe, or *tomol*, built by the Chumash Maritime Association. The oarsmen are, from left to right, Oscar Ortiz, Steven Villa, Mati Waiya, and Perry Cabugos.

Plate 12. Low tide at Home Bay, as seen from the Estero Trail above Drakes Estero, or estuary, at Point Reyes National Seashore, California.

Plate 13. Pomo dancers performing during a Kuksu secret society ceremony. The artist, Mort Künstler, based his reconstruction on dance regalia in the collections of the Phoebe A. Hearst Museum of Anthropology.

Plate 14. A painting by Luke Wisner showing what a typical Tongva village on Ballona Lagoon might have looked like in the past.

Plate 15. Russell A. Ruiz, *Chumash Indian Village with Canoes*, possibly painted in the 1960s. A second village sits on the clifftop in the left background.

Plate 16. Archaeologist Dale Clawson records a bedrock milling feature at Anza Borrego State Park, San Diego County. In basins ground into bedrock, California Indians pulverized seeds and other plant foods before cooking them.

Plate 17. David W. Rickman, *Chumash Canoe Makers at Carpenteria*. In 1769 Juan Crespí named the site of the present-day city of Carpinteria for the Chumash carpenters who were making plank boats there. These builders are caulking the seams between planks with naturally occurring tar.

Plate 18. Pool Rock, a Chumash rock art site that became a popular destination following publication of its location in several hiking guides. Staff of the Los Padres National Forest had to close the site for its protection.

Plate 19. Winged dancer painted at Burro Flats.

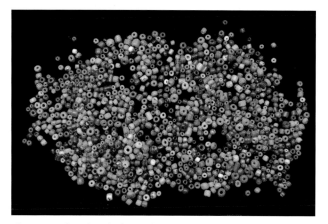

Plate 20. Glass beads from the Santa Barbara Channel region.

Plate 21. Naturalistic painting of a California condor, with its distinctive red head. The bird, which gives Condor Cave its popular name, is painted over a large bear paw petroglyph.

Plate 22. Autumn sunset at Baker Beach, San Francisco.

Plate 23. Elephant seals bask on the beach at Piedras Blancas, near San Simeon, California.

Plate 24. Salt marsh at Drakes Estero, Point Reyes National Seashore, California. The first coastal Californians used tule reeds like these to make boats and thatched houses.

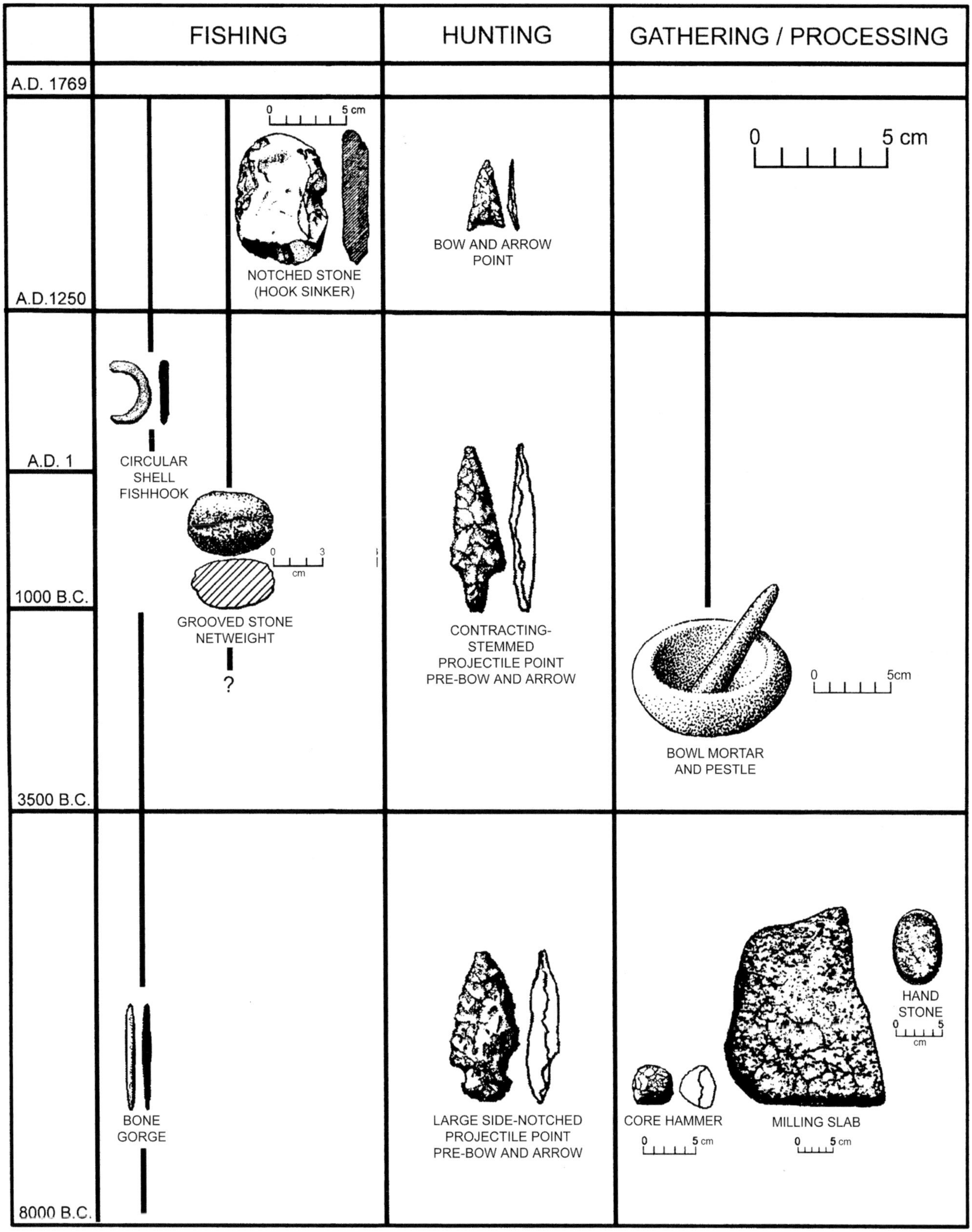

Figure 7.5. Common hunting, fishing, and plant-processing artifacts from the central California coast.

Although the lifeway now emphasized hunting, the acorn harvest must have been the big event in the fall, a time when men, women, and children ventured inland to collect nuts. Storage granaries became regular features in villages. Nearby, women carried out their daily routines of grinding and leaching the nuts. (Acorns contain large amounts of tannic acid, which must be removed by leaching, or straining the ground meal with water—a process not unlike making coffee, except that in this case the "grounds," not the liquid, are the desired end product.) Men were gone from the village more often, hunting deer and elk.

Why lifeways shifted at this time is a matter of debate. There is some evidence that the climate finally began to cool after a long Early Holocene warm period, when California was warmer and drier than it is today. Cooling would have promoted larger populations of game animals and encouraged more hunting. Evidence also exists that new waves of immigrants made their ways into central California around fifty-five hundred years ago, so in some places, such as the Monterey Bay area, changes in the economy also reflect the arrival of new ethnic groups.

Trade increased noticeably at this time, too, as we see from an increase in obsidian artifacts in archaeological sites. This shiny volcanic glass, from which knappers flaked much sharper spear points, knives, and scrapers than they could with locally available chert, came only from sources in the eastern Sierra Nevada and the San Francisco Bay area, two hundred to three hundred miles away. Most likely, no one trader traveled any great distance to obtain obsidian. Rather, people probably passed pieces of the stone from one village to the next and the next, until they ultimately reached faraway users. Tiny quantities of obsidian in Milling Stone sites suggest that such exchange took place occasionally as early as ten thousand years ago, but after fifty-five hundred years ago people regularly acquired obsidian for the hunting and butchering tools so important to them.

Between fifty-five hundred and one thousand years ago, even while hunters tracked deer and elk, their fellow villagers on the central coast increasingly fished in nearshore waters. After about three thousand years ago, they were aided by a new innovation, the circular shell fishhook. Before these hooks appeared, central coast fishers had caught nearshore fish using

Figure 7.6. Indians hunting with a bow and arrows above San Francisco Bay. Lithographic reproduction of an 1816 drawing by Louis Choris.

straight bone pieces, called gorges, attached to lines and bait. The new hooks, made from abalone or mussel shells, were almost certainly more effective for keeping fish on the line. With hooks and nets—the latter represented archaeologically by fist-size grooved stones believed to have been net weights—people caught most of the species of nearshore fish that can be seen in the Monterey Bay Aquarium today, including rockfish, sardines, surfperch, and cabezon.

Between roughly 1,000 and 750 years ago, much of California experienced prolonged droughts during a warm period that some scientists call the Medieval Climatic Anomaly. With a large array of food resources to choose from, especially marine animals, people of the central coast capably withstood these droughts, although occasionally they abandoned villages in poorly watered locations in favor of places adjacent to bigger creeks and stronger springs.

In the midst of the droughts came another dramatic change—the appearance of a powerful new weapon, the bow and arrow. We do not know exactly where the bow originated in North America, and it seems to have arrived in some parts of California slightly earlier than in others. But because it was such an enormous improvement over its predecessor, the atlatl, people embraced it quickly. On the central coast the bow and arrow took hold as the weapon of choice by eight hundred years ago, and it is after that time

Figure 7.7. The southern shoreline of Monterey Bay today, looking east with the Santa Lucia Range in the background.

At the time Fields wrote, the dwindling Native populations of Monterey Bay and other parts of the central coast had for 150 years forcibly shared their home-land with Spaniards, who established Mission San Carlos in Carmel in 1770, six other missions between 1771 and 1791, the Presidio, or fort, at Monterey in 1770, and the Pueblo de Branciforte, adja-cent to Mission Santa Cruz, in 1797. From the perspective of the indigenous people,

that we can directly connect the archaeological record with the peoples whom the Spaniards later described. By 750 years ago, all ten languages recorded histori-cally were being spoken on the coast by people who processed acorns; hunted large and small game with bows and arrows; collected abalones, mussels, clams, and many other shellfish; and caught virtually all species of nearshore fish using shell hooks, nets, and tule balsa canoes.

Adding to the multiculturalism of the central coast, people from California's great Central Valley—not unlike some of the visitors to the Monterey Bay Aquarium in 2013—journeyed seasonally to the shore to enjoy a little time in the sunshine. Historical accounts such as one written in 1924 by Stephen Fields, a long-time resident of the Monterey coast (published in the journal *American Anthropologist* in 1950), suggest that the Yokuts, or Tulares, who spoke a language different from that of the resident Ohlone people, visited the coast near Monterey with an inter-est in the seashore: "The Tulares came once a year and bathed in Monterey Bay and scraped their skin. They stayed about two weeks. They fought with the Carmel Indians when they came. The Tulares took back mus-sels and abalones."

events of the intervening decades cannot be cast in a favorable light. The newest group to arrive on the central coast, by sea and by land, carried racism and disregard for the cultures, traditions, and intelligence of those who had settled there long before. Some of the Spanish padres may have had what they believed to be good intentions in trying to convert California Indians to Catholicism, but the establishment of the missions and the reorganization of Native communities in mission compounds brought about rampant disease, deaths, and severe population decline (chapter 14). As Stephen Fields's account suggests, the arrival of new groups in the pre-Columbian past might not always have been conflict free, and pre-Columbian burials testify to occasional violence in central California. Yet the catastrophic events that followed the arrival of Spaniards were wholly unprecedented in the pre-ceding thirteen thousand years of human history on the central coast. In the end, happily, Native people did not vanish, and today their descendants, though outnumbered by millions of subsequent immigrants, remain a visible presence on a coast that continues to draw people of different cultural backgrounds to its shores.

Figure 8.1. Western Santa Cruz Island.

Ten Thousand Years on the Northern Channel Islands

Jennifer E. Perry, Michael A. Glassow, Torben C. Rick, and Jon M. Erlandson

Ten miles into our ocean journey from Ventura Harbor, we gaze through the salt spray at boats of all sizes, from yachts to tankers, and at a line of oil platforms off the California coast. The Santa Barbara Channel teems with life. Dolphins surf in the wake of our craft, the *Island Adventure*, which transports people and cargo to and from the northern Channel Islands. We are traveling to Prisoners Harbor on Santa Cruz Island, the largest of the eight Channel Islands. After the noise of the towns and highways along the mainland coast, the islands at first seem deceptively quiet. They are managed by the National Park Service, the US Navy, and private organizations such as the Nature Conservancy; the only one with permanent residents today is Catalina, one of the southern islands.

When Juan Rodríguez Cabrillo, captain of the first Spanish fleet to explore the coast of California, anchored off the Channel Islands in 1542, he saw a different scene. Chumash Indians lived on the northern islands and Tongva Indians on the southern islands— thousands of people with thriving, ocean-based economies. Chumash and Tongva artisans and traders were among many who participated in exchange networks that had crisscrossed southern California for millennia. In return for mainland products such as plant foods and baskets, islanders supplied mainlanders with dried fish, sea otter pelts, and beads made from seashells, some of which California Indians used as a currency into historic times (chapter 12).

Island dwellers carried these goods from one island to another or from islands to the mainland by boat. The Chumash probably built different kinds of boats at different times in their history, but for fifteen hundred years or more the plank canoe, or *tomol* in their language, was the mainstay of the island economy. In terms of labor and materials, tomols are expensive to construct, and their builders need special knowledge and experience. Unlike car ownership today, when thousands of personal vehicles congest the highways of southern California, boat ownership among the Chumash was limited to the few traders and chiefs who could afford it. Differences in wealth and status were a fact of life for Channel Islanders, and people gained affluence and prestige through personal

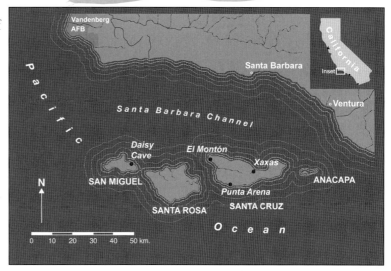

Figure 8.2. The Santa Barbara Channel and the archaeological sites Daisy Cave, Punta Arena, El Montón, and Xaxas.

accomplishments, trade, and inheritance along family lines (chapter 10).

On Santa Cruz Island, in excavations at the village of Xaxas (Sandy Place) at Prisoners Harbor, archaeologists have found evidence of Chumash life over the past three thousand years—the Late Holocene geological epoch. Xaxas housed fishers, traders, political leaders, and makers of shell bead money. In and around their village they discarded spent tools and debris from bead making alongside the trash of everyday life, until it eventually piled up as a large shell midden, or heap composed of shells, bones, artifacts, and other ancient refuse. Island middens range from small scatters of shell just a few inches thick to huge deposits like the one at Xaxas, as many as ten feet deep.

Elite households at Xaxas enjoyed access to mainland products and high-status foods such as swordfish. One such elite family built its house, later excavated by Jeanne Arnold, with some of the highly coveted redwood that washed down to the Channel Islands from California's mainland coast. Canoe builders, too, preferred redwood for making the tomols that they and others paddled through the waters around Xaxas. This village seems to have been one of the major economic ports on the northern islands.

Today's boat passengers stand mesmerized along the *Island Adventure*'s railings, watching the island grow larger. Approaching the pier at Prisoners Harbor, the engines slow and we land and transfer our gear from the boat to trucks. On a slow, dusty drive to the west end of the island, we snake up and down ridgelines in four-wheel drive. We navigate creek beds, watch birds, and notice native plants including oaks, pines, sage scrub, and the flowers of edible bulbs. We follow the paths of those who came before us—ranchers, wine makers, Chinese abalone fishers, and the Chumash. Our thoughts drift deeper into the past, back to when people first arrived on the northern Channel Islands, some thirteen thousand years ago.

The islands today look very different from the way they did then. Until about ten thousand years ago, lower sea levels joined the four northern islands—San Miguel, Santa Rosa, Santa Cruz, and Anacapa—into a single landmass, Santarosae. Just a handful of archaeological sites represents the earliest human occupation of the Channel Islands (chapter 2); the number of sites dating after about eleven thousand years ago is

Figure 8.3. A bundle of sea grass cordage, approximately one and a half inches wide, excavated at Daisy Cave on San Miguel Island.

dramatically larger. Dozens of shell middens, stone tool quarries and workshops, and cave sites that are between 10,500 and 8,000 years old have been identified on San Miguel, Santa Rosa, and Santa Cruz Islands. Islanders at that time used boats and other technologies to harvest fish, shellfish, seals, sea lions, aquatic birds, and terrestrial plants. Recent archaeological research has greatly improved our understanding of these early people and their environment.

One of the places where early Channel Islanders lived was Daisy Cave on San Miguel Island. For millennia this small cave sheltered people from storms and the strong winds that often sweep San Miguel. Jon Erlandson and his team of archaeologists have uncovered in Daisy Cave an amazing record of environmental changes and of human diet and technology spanning the past 11,500 years. Today, San Miguel is a wilderness, with only a handful of trails and no wheeled vehicles, so to reach Daisy Cave the crew had to hike six miles every day over high dunes, through thick vegetation, and against high winds, often carrying heavy equipment or samples. Their treks were worth the effort, for the site has reshaped archaeologists' understanding of the ancient Channel Islands.

As people discarded animal bones, seashells, and artifacts in Daisy Cave, the refuse from different time periods became discrete layers, or strata, somewhat

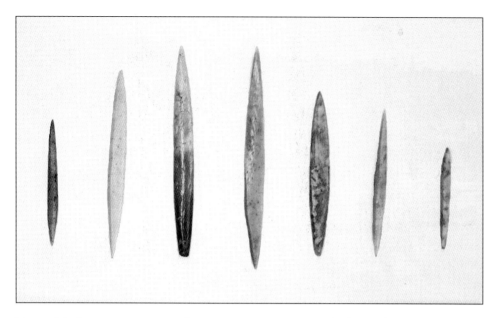

Figure 8.4. Bone gorges excavated at Daisy Cave on San Miguel Island. The middle gorge is 1.3 inches long.

like the layers of a cake. Each layer, when carefully excavated, provides a glimpse into the Channel Islands' deep history. Because families sought shelter in Daisy Cave, a choice that helped preserve rare artifacts that would have rotted away in the open air, archaeologists have uncovered hundreds of pieces of cordage and a fragment of a nine-thousand-year-old child's sandal woven from sea grass. They also found an unusual crescent-shaped stone tool and a kind of spear point called the Channel Island Barbed point (see figs. 2.4–2.6), distinctive artifacts that islanders used between about twelve thousand and eight thousand years ago as part of a sophisticated maritime hunting tool kit. Small, toothpick-like bone gorges found in the cave are among the oldest fishhooks in the Americas. Thousands of fish, bird, and mammal bones, along with shellfish, demonstrate that early residents relied on ocean foods, especially fish.

Along with Daisy Cave, dozens of smaller open-air sites enhance our understanding of the early people who lived on the northern Channel Islands. Although their lives were attuned to the sea, it is increasingly clear that they also made good use of terrestrial plants. Early islanders moved from place to place, laying the foundation for the ensuing millennia of human habitation.

On a pleasant summer day in 1981, Mike Glassow stood at the edge of an eight-foot-deep test pit that a crew of students had excavated into El Montón, a huge shell midden near the west end of Santa Cruz Island. El Montón had risen through centuries of human use between about fifty-eight hundred and twenty-five hundred years ago, during the Middle Holocene. The pit walls exposed several recognizable strata. The uppermost layer, nearly three feet thick, consisted mostly of fragmented mussel shells. Below that lay sand from an ancient dune, which extended to the base of the pit. Within the sand ran two thin layers rich in large red abalone shells, some of them ten inches long.

Why did these two layers contain so many red abalone shells while the deposits above them did not? Almost every site on the island contains lots of mussel shell, but few have much red abalone shell. Carl Hubbs, an oceanographer who visited the Channel Islands in the 1950s, proposed an explanation for this. He reasoned that island shell middens containing red abalone were deposited at times when seawater temperatures were cooler than today's. When water was warmer, red abalones lived only in deeper water, which would have been relatively inaccessible from shore. When the temperature of intertidal and shallow waters cooled, red abalones would have been able to survive in those zones, and islanders could have collected them from shore at low tide.

Figure 8.5. Excavations at the Punta Arena site on Santa Cruz Island.

mound ?

If we follow Hubbs's argument, then the occupants at El Montón who discarded the red abalone shells in the lowermost layers had relatively easy access to these marine snails. The later occupants did not, so the upper layers they created lack red abalone shells. Evidence from the Channel Islands farther west, Santa Rosa and San Miguel, supports aspects of Hubbs's explanation. Waters around those islands have always been cooler than waters around Santa Cruz Island, home of El Montón, and we now know of many red abalone middens on Santa Rosa and San Miguel. Clearly, red abalones were accessible to islanders there throughout the Middle Holocene.

Conversely, waters around central and eastern Santa Cruz Island (El Montón sits at the northwestern tip) were too warm during the later part of the Middle Holocene for red abalones to be collected near shore. Archaeological sites of this period on most of Santa Cruz Island lack red abalone shells. The red abalone middens on western Santa Cruz, including the two layers at El Montón, all date between seven thousand and fifty-three hundred years ago, when local waters

must have been cool. The small sizes of most of the red abalone middens, less than seventy-five feet in diameter, imply that people moved from one camp to another during much of the year, staying only long enough at each camp—perhaps just a few weeks—to acquire, consume, and discard the refuse of the most accessible red abalones and other shellfish. A few red abalone middens, such as that at the Punta Arena site, are much larger. Islanders clearly spent a lot more time at these places, acquiring other marine foods such as fish and sea mammals, notably dolphins. A stone mortar and pestle found at one of the smaller red abalone middens suggests that people also collected seeds or nuts and crushed them into flour.

The small number of sites dating to the Middle Holocene and their small sizes tell us that island groups of the time were smaller and moved around more than later populations. Besides collecting shellfish, people occasionally fished and hunted sea mammals. They dug for root crops using digging sticks with doughnut-shaped stone weights wedged onto the shafts, as their descendants would continue

Figure 8.6. A digging stick weight, four and a half inches in diameter, from the Santa Barbara Channel region.

to do throughout the rest of pre-Columbian times. We suspect that the most important root crop was blue dicks, which is widespread on the islands. Blue dicks plants grow from tasty, carbohydrate-rich corms (similar to bulbs) that can be eaten cooked or raw.

Over time, islanders changed their economic strategies. They abandoned many of the sites with red abalone middens and, especially on Santa Cruz Island, turned their attention to the islands' interiors for foods with which to complement their seafood diet. They may have done so in response to rising ocean temperatures, which by four thousand years ago were warmer than at any other time during the Holocene, and to heavier rainfall, which favored the abundance of edible plants. Not surprisingly, archaeologists often find the hallmark artifacts of plant processing—stone mortars and pestles—at interior island sites, and craftspeople now made these tools more carefully than they had during earlier periods.

Yet islanders still spent time at the shore. The large sizes of some seaside archaeological sites and their association with cemeteries imply that people continued to gather periodically on the coast. Moving between coastal and inland locations is one example of the way islanders successfully adjusted to a changing environment by adapting their diet and their use of diverse island landscapes. Judging from similarities in the material culture of earlier and later sites, as well as from genetic data, the people who made these changes were the direct ancestors of the Chumash people whom the Spaniards met. Indeed, current evidence suggests that cultural continuity endured on the northern islands for seventy-five hundred years or longer.

The past three thousand years witnessed growth in the populations and economies of peoples along the Santa Barbara Channel. Some of the larger coastal villages that islanders established, such as Syuxtun at Santa Barbara, remained home to craft specialists, boat owners, shamans, and chiefs well into the Spanish colonial years. Although the Chumash continued to collect plants and shellfish, they stepped up their fishing and trading. In contrast to the moving around of earlier times, islanders now lived full-time in larger, more crowded villages positioned near sandy beaches suitable for launching and landing boats (plate 15), such as the beach at Prisoners Harbor. Larger populations meant that a group could no longer move easily into a new area; another group likely was already living there. So islanders experienced greater hardships when droughts struck and they could not relocate to find water. Sometimes, friction within or between crowded villages led to violence. Fernando Librado Kitsepawit, the son of a Chumash couple from Santa Cruz Island, told the anthropologist John P. Harrington of a time when civil war erupted there because of a dispute over who should inherit the role of paramount chief.

Following the coastal Indians' first contact with Europeans in 1542, many of them died from introduced diseases to which they had no immunity. By the 1820s all the surviving Channel Islanders had been relocated to missions on the mainland nearby (plate 3), bringing an end to some thirteen thousand years of sustained habitation of the Channel Islands. Although the accounts are not perfect, mission records and details recorded by John Harrington from interviews with Chumash descendants help greatly in reconstructing the late pre-Columbian and historical peoples and villages on the islands.

Anthropologist John Johnson has pored over these records and learned that some twenty named

Figure 8.7. House depressions and accumulated shell midden at site SCRI-195 on Santa Cruz Island.

villages, including Xaxas, existed on the islands of San Miguel, Santa Rosa, and Santa Cruz before 1820. An 1805 letter from the head of the California missions to the Spanish governor describes how Chumash from different villages gathered in large numbers to attend feasts on Santa Cruz Island. People came from other island and mainland villages and towns, walking and paddling along routes that Chumash descendants now retrace in an annual gathering of the Chumash Maritime Association.

Archaeologists have discovered the probable locations of most of the villages Johnson identified, along with smaller sites that attest to the way whole communities once thrived on the Channel Islands. Often, former Chumash villages on the northern islands are now spectacular archaeological sites with middens more than ten feet deep. Where Chumash families lived for centuries or even millennia, excavators typically find large, circular depressions—the remnants of houses—where residents left signs of the full range of their lifeways. There are everyday items such as circular shell fishhooks, stone bowls, and baskets—things used in fishing, hunting, and cooking. There are cemeteries and sometimes evidence of feasts, rituals, and ceremonies. Each village was politically

Figure 8.8. Wooden bowl with shell bead inlay, collected in the late 1870s by Leon de Cessac in the Santa Barbara Channel region. Indians living along the channel made bowls from materials including stone, wood, and whale bone, inlaying some of them with shell beads, which increased their value.

independent, but people everywhere stayed connected through marriage, trade, and a ritual organization known as the 'antap (chapter 11). Visiting the remaining shell middens, now protected by law from any digging or collecting without a permit, is a remarkable experience, for they conjure up images of once vibrant communities in places now returned to wilderness.

After finishing our excavations, we pack our midden samples, equipment, and camp trash in the trucks. Before winding our way back across the island terrain, we take one last look at the place that was our home for the past few weeks and reflect on how we have retraced the footsteps of those who lived there during the past thousands of years. Arriving at Prisoners Harbor, we load our gear onto the pier to await the return voyage to the mainland. Sitting on the sandy beach, before the exhaust and roar of the *Island Adventure* again bombards our senses, we can almost smell the cooking fires at Xaxas, recalling earlier days when tomols regularly crossed these waters.

Figure 9.1. Aerial view of the Ballona wetland area of Los Angeles, 1950s.

People of the Ballona

John G. Douglass, Jeffrey H. Altschul, Donn R. Grenda, Seetha N. Reddy,
and Richard Ciolek-Torello

Anyone who has driven in Los Angeles knows "the 405," an interstate freeway paralleling the Pacific Ocean coastline and linking the San Fernando Valley to southern Orange County. For much of its length the 405 slices through a dense, urban, concrete jungle. It wasn't always this way. Where vast agricultural fields once lay, huge residential developments sprang up after World War II. Most Angelinos believe the sprawl of the west side destroyed their history. But they're wrong—much of the past is still preserved, waiting to be rediscovered. American Indian place-names such as Topanga, Malibu, Azusa, Simi, and Cucamonga furnish tantalizing clues to who lived there, although few Angelinos give them a second thought.

Over the past thirty years, we have painstakingly uncovered parts of Los Angeles's past through archaeology. We have made exciting and unusual finds among, in-between, and below the urban sprawl of the twentieth century. Key among these finds are the archaeological remains of the Ballona, a landscape so transformed from its long-ago state that when we first saw it in the late 1980s, it more closely resembled an urban wasteland than the thriving wetlands it had been for nearly eight thousand years.

Nestled along Santa Monica Bay just north of Los Angeles International Airport, the dynamic wetland called the Ballona evolved over thousands of

years from an open bay of the Pacific to a sediment-filled coastal lagoon. Long before Howard Hughes leveled portions of the wetland to build military aircraft during and after World War II, long before Marina del Rey became a harbor for the rich and famous in the 1960s, and long before the modern community of Playa Vista emerged from the lagoon in the 1990s, the Ballona was home to American Indians, the most recent of whom were the Tongva. We don't know what the Natives called the wetlands; perhaps it was Sa'an, a place-name recorded by the anthropologist Alfred Kroeber in the early twentieth century. By Kroeber's time, though, the area was known locally as the Ballona. The name might be a misspelling of the Spanish word *ballena*, which translates as "whale," or

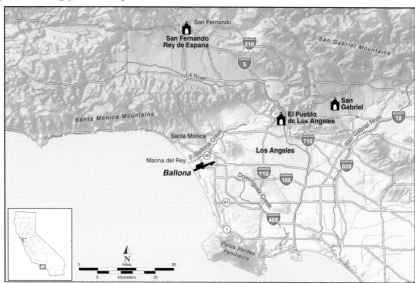

Figure 9.2. Location of the Ballona along Santa Monica Bay in west Los Angeles. Area of intense archaeological investigations is shaded.

it might have been derived from *Bayona*, the region of Spain in which one of the early ranching families, the Talamantes, originated. No one knows.

Like so many of southern California's other coastal lagoons, the Ballona tells a story of great cultural and natural transformation. Humans came to the Ballona to enjoy its bounty. Archaeological sites cover every hillock and rise on the Westchester Bluffs, which form the physical southern margin of the Ballona, and along a nearly continuous two-mile stretch at the base of the bluffs adjacent to small but perennial Centinela Creek. Although archaeologists and history buffs had long known about and investigated the sites on the bluff tops, those at the base of the bluffs remained largely undiscovered and untouched until we first spied the area in 1989. Glimpses of sites were visible in narrow strips of native soil at the edges of parking lots and along roads. Soil cores showed us that although Hughes destroyed some archaeological sites, he probably saved many more by burying them under vast amounts of fill. We focused our work at the base of the bluffs. There we uncovered marvelous things that, when pieced together, helped write a lost chapter of Los Angeles's history.

Eight thousand years ago the Ballona would have looked very different from the way it does today, even without modern development. Imagine yourself standing on a high point then, overlooking the area. Sea level is much lower than it is now, because glacial ice still locks up vast amounts of water. Ocean waves crash on an open beach hundreds of yards farther from shore than today's beaches. To the north glitters a narrow bay fed by a cobble-strewn stream whose many rivulets twist and turn around sand islands and marshes as they enter the bay. Thousands of years later the stream will be named Ballona Creek. Beyond the small marsh at the mouth of the creek, a wide coastal plain clad in grasses and shrubs stretches for several miles to the north and east. Turning around, you look south over a vast coastal prairie dotted with vernal pools, seasonally water-filled depressions that hold and attract an array of plants and animals. You and your family—among the first humans to arrive in the Ballona—have come here to hunt, fish, and gather plants for a few days or weeks before exhausting the resources and moving on.

And so the Ballona remained for thousands of years. Sea levels rose as ice turned to water. Around five thousand years ago sea levels largely stabilized, and the main force shaping the Ballona shifted from the ocean to the rivers feeding it. Today Ballona Creek is a concrete channel, draining a small part of west Los Angeles, but for much of the last eight thousand years the creek was the main course of the Los Angeles River. As the mountains inland eroded, sediment flowed down the river and emptied into the Ballona, eventually transforming the open coast into a freshwater lagoon by approximately fifty-seven hundred years ago.

Around the lagoon, natural plant and animal communities became larger and more diverse, eventually attracting humans to settle in the Ballona for longer and longer periods. Around two thousand years ago, the temporary camps of hunters and fishermen gave way to small villages. The area on the south side of the lagoon became a hotbed of community activity. Residents placed their villages on the bluff tops, overlooking the lagoon, where they launched tule boats, cleaned fish, shucked oysters, opened clams, and hunted the birds and other animals of the marsh.

No one knows who the first inhabitants of the Ballona were or what they called their villages, but around thirty-five hundred years ago they acquired new neighbors: Tongva people who moved in south of the villages to collect plants and hunt small animals on the rich coastal prairie (plate 14). By the time hunting camps gave way to villages around the lagoon, the ancestors of the modern Tongva had made their way into the Los Angeles Basin and the Ballona, as well as onto the southern Channel Islands. By about two thousand years ago, village patterns looked similar all across the region. Yet the Ballona economy was decidedly local, making the most of immediately available, nearby resources. In contrast, the Tongva's better-known northern neighbors, the Chumash, made their living by fishing, mainly for offshore fish, and by hunting sea mammals.

What were the Ballona villages like? In Los Angeles, archaeologists usually are able to excavate only tiny parts of villages, but we were fortunate to get to excavate one of them, the Del Rey site (LAN-63), almost completely. Situated on the bluff overlooking the Ballona, the Del Rey site was highly organized. Its Tongva residents set aside different portions of their village for different activities. They dug hearths, or fire

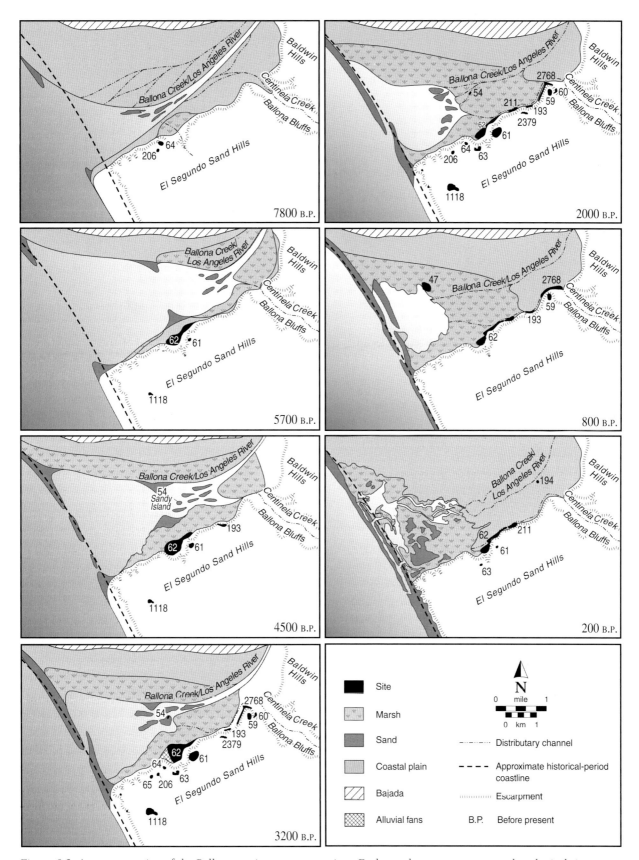

Figure 9.3. A reconstruction of the Ballona environment over time. Each number represents an archaeological site.

Figure 9.4. Excavation of one of two pits identified at the Del Rey site in which villagers buried intentionally broken objects during communal mourning rituals. Part of a stone pestle is visible in the foreground.

Figure 9.5. A six-foot-long stone pestle found in the second of the ceremonial pits at the Del Rey site. This pestle was manufactured only for ritual use and was purposefully broken during the ancient mourning rite.

pits, in an arc bordering a large open area in the center of the village. Each hearth likely served an ancient household that also had a windbreak or a shallow house pit with a house superstructure composed of perishable materials such as reeds and grasses, which have long since decomposed. Around the hearths, people cooked, fashioned stone tools, and repaired and waterproofed bowls and baskets with asphaltum, a naturally occurring tar.

In the center of the village, residents held communal mourning rituals during which they purposely broke the possessions of the dead and other objects created specially for ritual destruction. Mourners sprinkled red ochre, a mineral pigment not found

locally, on the funeral objects and splattered asphaltum on them. Afterward, they placed the broken objects in a pit in the middle of the village and buried them. Many tribes throughout southern California practiced communal mourning rites as late as the end of the nineteenth century or into the early twentieth century, but finding archaeological evidence of the rituals is rare.

What did Ballona villagers eat? Fish and shellfish from the nearby lagoon were the mainstays of the diet, as they had been for thousands of years. Also popular with early villagers were small mammals such as rabbits and rodents. Not only was their meat important, but so was their extremely nutritious bone marrow. In middens, archaeologists find many small mammal bones crushed and pulverized, the result of people's getting to the marrow inside. Hunters took occasional large mammals such as deer, but their meat did not make up a large part of the diet. Nuts, seeds, and tubers, in contrast, were very important. Because some key plant foods, such as native acorns and walnuts, grew farther inland, villagers likely spent part of the year elsewhere, collecting these seasonal resources to bring back to their primary homes in the Ballona.

When Spaniards established a presence in California in the late 1700s, they viewed the landscape as wild and untamed. Nothing could have been further from the truth. Native Californians, including the Tongva, managed and altered the landscapes they inhabited for their own needs. They encouraged some resources, overexploited others, and neglected still others. Far from being passive agents who simply reacted to environmental change, California tribes actively manipulated and managed the landscape in many ways. They used fire, for example, as a tool with which to effectively manage grasslands, forests, groves, and wetlands (chapter 4). In the Ballona area, it is likely—although we have no direct evidence—that people similarly altered the wetlands and adjacent coastal prairie. The wetlands adjacent to many of the Ballona villages provided food—fish, shellfish, migratory birds—and materials for making baskets, watercraft, and housing. By regularly burning the wetlands, residents cleared out dead plants and encouraged new growth.

It was not just fire that the people of the Ballona kept in their tool kit. Hunter-gatherers are keen observers of changes in plants and animals. Plants, in particular, can be manipulated, and if manipulated in the right ways, they become domesticates. The Kumeyaay Indians, for example, who lived farther south, toward the San Diego area, may have irrigated stands of wild plants. An examination of preserved seeds from excavated Ballona sites shows that the Tongva may have selected plants with larger seeds than others. By collecting plants with larger seeds and then sowing them in the coastal prairie, perhaps the Tongva were taking the first steps toward plant domestication.

One site in the Ballona, LAN-62, housed first living residents and later the deceased almost continuously for seven thousand years—well into the Spanish mission years. Repeatedly, people came to this place on a dry, elevated landform just above the lagoon to fish, hunt birds, and collect plants and shellfish in the marshes and lagoon. Gradually, they piled up a thick midden with their refuse. Around a thousand years ago, for reasons unknown, people stopped living at LAN-62 and transformed it into a place of the dead. By the late 1700s the site had become a formal burial ground, with upright whale bones marking the graves and probably a wooden fence around the outside. Most of the people buried there likely lived and died at Guaspet, which historical records reveal to have been the main indigenous village of the Ballona. Even natives of Guaspet who married into other villages, some as far away as Santa Catalina Island, may have been carried back to be buried at LAN-62.

Analysis of the burials and the items interred with them suggests a strong connection between Native residents of the Ballona and the newly arrived Hispanic colonists living at the Pueblo de Los Angeles, Missions San Gabriel and San Fernando Rey, and local ranchos. Mission baptismal records reveal that ninety-two members of the village of Guaspet were recruited to the missions and baptized. Many of the deceased buried at LAN-62 were accompanied in their graves by a mix of traditional Tongva-manufactured goods and items obtained through trade or interaction with colonists. When burials contained European items, they were combined in a way that expressed traditional Native values. Some Tongva buried at LAN-62 probably worked at local ranchos, such as Rancho Los Quintos; their graves contained objects associated with cowboys and ranch hands. Many of the graves held glass beads, which colonists and local inhabitants used as a medium of exchange.

Just west of the burials at LAN-62 is an area we believe was dedicated to a mourning ceremony not unlike the ones held at the older Del Rey site, but in this case performed during the mission period. In the historical Tongva mourning ceremony, as early ethnographers documented it, participants burned and ritually destroyed personal items of the dead or items specially created for the ceremony, just as they did at the Del Rey site centuries before. At LAN-62 we found a series of small pits containing the burned remains of broken stone tools, baskets, large amounts of seeds,

Figure 9.6. Artist's reconstruction of the burial area at LAN-62.

and shell and glass beads. Many of the seeds offered were traditional native ones rather than foods introduced by Spanish colonialists.

Two likely reasons for the creation of the sacred burial area were the antiquity of the site and people's collective memory of their ancestors. LAN-62 has the longest occupational history of any archaeological site in the Ballona. Later users of the place retained some sort of social memory of its ancient inhabitants, as we see from their having placed in mission-period burials some special grave goods much older than the deceased themselves. These artifacts must have been either unearthed by later people from older portions of the site or passed down in families over the generations as heirlooms. Remembrance of the site's long history and deep, intricate web of human relationships helped the people of the Ballona connect with their past and face their future.

For thousands of years, little changed in the everyday lives of people in the Ballona. Then, suddenly, the

arrival of Spanish colonists disrupted their traditional ways. Many of the people buried at LAN-62 had interacted with the newly arrived colonizers as the latter established missions and ranchos outside the Ballona. They acquired new, exotic items even while doing their best to maintain traditional rituals, festivals, and other aspects of Tongva culture. But theirs was a losing battle, and by the early nineteenth century the Native communities of the Ballona and elsewhere around Mission San Gabriel had been incorporated into ranchos.

Tongva culture has persisted to this day, but in time the old village names grew hazy and were mostly forgotten, except in oral traditions and cryptic references on historic maps. Industry replaced agriculture, and the Ballona lost any semblance of its marshes and wetlands. Yet with the aid of the science of archaeology and the memories of Tongva descendants, the story of the Ballona can once more be told.

Figure 9.7. Colonial-period items found at LAN-62, demonstrating the close interaction between Tongva residents of the Ballona and newly arrived Spanish colonists. *Clockwise from top left:* iron hoe head; salt-glazed stoneware child's or demitasse cup; string of glass beads; deformed copper chocolate pot (approximately four inches wide).

Figure 10.1. Rafael Solares, a Chumash chief and member of the *'antap* ceremonial society, 1878.

California Indian Chiefs and Other Elites

Lynn H. Gamble

On the afternoon of September 4, 1769, Father Juan Crespí met for the first time the imposing Chumash chief whom Spaniards called El Buchón. Crespí and the other men accompanying Gaspar de Portolá on the first European land expedition into California had trudged that morning through sand dunes near the modern town of Arroyo Grande, just south of San Luis Obispo. Crespí grumbled in his diary about sinking in the sand. After four hours of dunes and rough terrain, the men finally came upon a lush hollow graced by sycamores and live oaks at the juncture of two streams. There they were greeted by El Buchón, a tall man "of very majestic and grand appearance," distinguished by a large "tumor," or *buchón*—actually an old arrow wound—hanging from the side of his neck.

El Buchón treated the tired, hungry Spaniards to a feast: "a great many big bowls full of good gruels, a great many others full of very good mush, fresh deer meat, a few fresh fish, and a bowl of a sort of white pies." The food fed all sixty-four members of the expedition with some left over. According to Crespí, El Buchón wore a fine cape made of otter skin that covered him from neck to ankles. Heavily armed men accompanied him. Crespí was struck by the deference people paid to the chief. Greatly respected by the Chumash and surrounding Indian groups, El Buchón enjoyed fame reaching as far as the Santa Barbara Channel to the south and the Santa Lucia Mountains to the north. He was, Crespí said, greatly "feared, held in awe and obeyed."

Continuing in his diary—published centuries later in English as *A Description of Distant Roads*—

Crespí wrote of El Buchón that "many villages give him tribute, whatever seeds they harvest or gather from the fields, [and] whether they slaughter any meat or catch fish, they take it all—or so we understood—to his village, where he receives it and then they take back whatever he tells them to. In their [the Chumash Indians'] own fashion, he employs considerable pomp, and they bring a hide and lay it on the ground for him to sit down on. He has two brothers and two or three sons who are almost always with him, and no one sits down in front of him or his family unless ordered to."

Like El Buchón, other Chumash chiefs stood out in a crowd. Draped in otter skin capes, they wore their hair up, secured with delicately carved bone pins and large, inlaid chert knives. Chiefs looked very different from commoners, who often wore nothing but body paint and a few accoutrements. One of the best existing images of a Chumash chief is a photograph of Rafael Solares taken in 1878 by Leon de Cessac. Solares wears a necklace of beads and a skirt of milkweed fiber twisted with white down feathers. His spectacular headdress is fashioned from feathers topped with the tails of magpies. Painted stripes decorate his body, and he appears to be carrying a deer-hoof rattle in one hand and a staff in the other.

Chiefs in other parts of California, too, stood out easily from commoners. For example, we know what chiefs and elite dancers in the San Francisco Bay area looked like from the exquisite watercolors painted in 1816 by Louis Choris, who accompanied Lieutenant Otto von Kotzebue to California as the expedition artist for the 1815–1818 Russian voyage to the Americas.

In the painting reproduced as figure 10.2, Choris depicts dancers, perhaps some of whom were chiefs. Two of the three men are adorned with necklaces made from shell beads and ornaments. They all wear ornate headdresses of feathers and bone pins. Choris's painting matches early written descriptions of high-status Indians from many parts of coastal California. We know from the observations of explorers and early anthropologists that chiefs ranked highest in prestige, followed by ritual leaders and others serving in ceremonial roles. All these elites dressed differently from commoners.

Figure 10.2. Native dancers in the San Francisco Bay area, wearing traditional headdresses and necklaces. Watercolor by Louis Choris, 1816.

Two of the most arresting images of California Indian elites are photographs of Captain Tom Lewis, a Nisenan chief living in Auburn, just northwest of Sacramento, and his wife, made by Alexander W. Chase in 1874. Although they represent inland peoples and not coastal tribes, they are among the earliest photographs of California Indians, taken at a time when the Nisenan still retained their traditional dress and ornaments. Captain Tom wears a brilliant red-colored flicker feather headband, a long wooden hairpin threaded with woodpecker scalps and flicker feathers, and a huge abalone shell pendant. Draped over his shoulders is a rabbit skin robe, which traditionally required more than forty rabbit pelts cut into strips and woven together. Captain Tom's wife, whose name is Jane, is adorned with a bead necklace ten yards long and made from approximately 1,160 clamshell beads. Her deerskin headband displays even more beads and worked abalone shells, as does her waistband. These rare images transport us back to a time when chiefs and their families proudly displayed their most prized possessions. Even in 1874, Captain Tom's and his wife's wearable wealth contrasted conspicuously with the plain clothing of Nisenan commoners, who in earlier times would have worn little or nothing at all.

Through these images we catch a glimpse of high-status persons who looked markedly different from most other people, but what about the rest of their lives—their power and privileges? One of the most significant rights of chiefs had to do with marriage. Male chiefs, unlike commoners, often took a second wife and sometimes a third. John Johnson, of the Santa Barbara Museum of Natural History, has delved into this issue with regard to the Chumash, spending countless hours studying antiquated, handwritten marriage records penned by Franciscan priests hundreds of years ago. The earliest mission records yield valuable information about the lives of the Chumash before their affiliation with Spanish missions, including details of traditional marriage and residence patterns. From these records, Johnson and other researchers can decipher who was married to whom, where the couples lived before and after marriage, who their parents were, and where the parents lived. Scholars have even identified the names and sexes of chiefs.

Mission records and early census records tell us that at least one chief, usually a man, governed most settlements. The smallest communities often lacked a chief, whereas two or more chiefs might govern the larger settlements. Along the Santa Barbara Channel, a chief's eldest son usually succeeded him as leader. Chiefly families intermarried widely, not unlike the royal families of Europe in the seventeenth and eighteenth centuries. By marrying one another, the daughters and sons of Chumash chiefs and other elites created strong trade partnerships and alignments that helped augment families' political power.

Figure 10.3. The Nisenan chief Captain Tom, of Auburn, California, wearing a rabbit fur robe and traditional head-dress, 1874.

Figure 10.4. Captain Tom's wife, Jane, wearing an enormous clamshell necklace, 1874.

Female chiefs, too, existed among Chumash groups. Juan Rodríguez Cabrillo, the first European explorer of California, described a female chief who ruled the sizable Chumash town of Syuxtun (plate 3), where Cabrillo spent three days in the fall of 1542. Syuxtun's Chumash residents welcomed the captain and his crew, supplying them with much-needed water and wood. The female chief, along with some other villagers, even spent a night on the ship. Through sign language, the elderly leader informed Cabrillo that she served as chief of a province stretch-ing from Syuxtun to Point Conception, roughly fifty miles northeast of today's Santa Barbara.

Because Cabrillo met this woman hundreds of years before whites settled in California, their

encounter shows that the existence of a female chief cannot be attributed to the effects of European coloni-zation and the breakdown of traditional positions of authority. That she oversaw a large Chumash area on the mainland attests to the position of power a woman could hold at the time. Female chiefs ruled into the colonial years as well. Records document one at the historic village of Shalawa, where Montecito sits today.

In the spring of 2012, a team of archaeology students and I had the opportunity to learn more about the historic Chumash village of Syuxtun. Once situated in a pristine setting overlooking a small cove on the Santa Barbara coastline, Syuxtun now lies cov-ered by modern buildings and a well-traveled coastal road in downtown Santa Barbara. Yet despite mod-ern development, remnants of the village can still be found. Our field class investigated Syuxtun by open-ing the floorboards of a historic building to determine whether or not the archaeological site was still intact. Digging three small pits, we found clear evidence of old Syuxtun. More than eight hundred shell and glass beads (plate 20), some so small that we captured them only by sieving the soil through a window screen, told

Figure 10.5. Excavations at Syuxtun, beneath the floor of an old house in Santa Barbara, 2012.

us that the village was founded at least a thousand years ago and remained a prominent Chumash center for decades after Spaniards arrived permanently in 1769. Besides the beads, we uncovered great quantities of bones from fish, sea mammals, and deer—all traces of sumptuous meals consumed by past inhabitants.

In addition to village chiefs, the Chumash recognized paramount chiefs, who possessed some authority—though not a great deal—over groups of settlements organized loosely into federations, often around a principal town. The female chief at Syuxtun may have been one of these, judging from the size of her domain. Using census records, archaeologists identify towns with more than one chief as political centers. These were places where people from smaller settlements came for ceremonies, to trade, and to coordinate activities with one another. Elites from political centers formed a network of coalitions in order to maintain their status, create alliances, and reinforce the power of their chiefs.

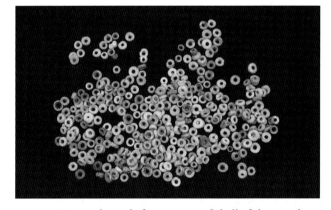

Figure 10.6. Beads made from pieces of shell of the purple olive (*Olivella* species), identical to beads found at Syuxtun. These came from the historic Chumash site of Kashtiq (CA-KER-307).

From John P. Harrington's obsessively comprehensive records, we know that Chumash chiefs, their family members, shamans, and other high-status persons served in a select group of religious and political specialists called the *'antap* society (chapter 11). In each major Chumash settlement, an *'antap* society presided over the affairs of the village, with the chief at the top of the hierarchy. Among other duties, *'antap* members performed dances and rituals at public ceremonies. Parents of children chosen as *'antap* paid dearly for the privilege with large quantities of shell bead money. The *'antap* organization functioned at both the village and provincial levels. Every few years, representatives of this elite council met in a capital town to oversee the political, ceremonial, and other business of the province.

The Chumash serve as only one example of the chiefdoms that once thrived along the California coast. Far to the north, around San Francisco Bay, chiefs also inherited their positions and were wealthier than everyone else, and male chiefs often married several women. The anthropologist W. C. McKern interviewed a number of Patwin Indians, members of a tribe living north of San Francisco Bay, and in 1922 wrote the following about chiefs, their wives, and their children in his book *Functional Families of the Patwin:* "They were freely supplied with the necessities of life by the other village members. For instance, if the chief needed firewood, he would call some of the young men to him and order them to get it for him. Or, when the time for harvesting a certain variety of grass seed was come, the chief's daughter, if of age, would call to her a number of the younger women and tell them she needed so many baskets of timothy grass seed, wild oats, or whatever the cereal might be." Indeed, the chief's daughters and sisters were so highly respected that children were even forbidden to laugh in their presence.

Patwin chiefs presided over ceremonies in great earth-covered dance houses. Within these cavernous structures, chiefs sat in their special place, the middle of the south side, surrounded by other elites who possessed power. Dance houses, the largest structures made by any California Indians, belonged to the chiefs. When chiefs died, they were often buried in the dance house and then it was burned.

Patwin chiefs apparently managed their people's economy closely. They assigned gathering areas to families each year according to their needs. On ceremonial occasions they gave away food that their people had earlier deposited with them. Chiefs also constructed, regulated, and operated fish weirs along the Sacramento River and its tributaries. Just to build a large weir—basically a dam with pens that captured salmon and other fish swimming upstream—required the chief to coordinate the labor of all the men in the settlement. Some weirs were so massive that several people could walk side by side across the river on them, as if on a bridge. Chiefs controlled the use of weirs and ensured that people upstream had a chance to share in the bounty of fish caught in the devices. Experts estimate that California Indians consumed more than fifteen million pounds of fish every year, much of which was dealt out by chiefs. Without careful coordination and respect for neighbors, conflicts could break out quickly. According to stories told by generations of Patwin, clashes often arose over people's taking resources from their neighbors. Chiefs took special care to ensure that everyone received an appropriate share of food and had no reason to feel outrage or jealousy.

Identifying chiefs in the archaeological record is far more difficult than interpreting early descriptions or deciphering mission records. Archaeologists can know little about individual chiefs' challenges, negotiations, successes, and failures, but we can identify the material emblems of high status in a cultural group, and sometimes they allow us to recognize individuals who must have been elites or even chiefs in life. One of the best places to look for evidence of high status is in the objects that California Indians buried in the graves of their dead.

More than a hundred years ago, collectors descended on the Santa Barbara area in search of fancy Chumash objects to place in emerging museums back east. In 1875 H. C. Yarrow led an expedition for the Smithsonian, and he and his team knew just where to look for museum-quality pieces. They and subsequent collectors headed straight for the ancient cemeteries to dig up burials. In the early twentieth century, researchers excavated Native burials more scientifically, but still with little regard for the concerns of California Indians. Today, archaeologists are appalled by these early investigators' disregard for the sanctity of the dead. Yet museums still house mortuary collections—now in consultation with Native groups and under legal mandates. With the permission of descendants, archaeologists are sometimes

Figure 10.7. Carved stone model of a canoe excavated by H. C. Yarrow.

allowed to study the old burial collections, in part for what they reveal about social inequality

Generally, archaeologists believe that persons into whose graves mourners placed fancy objects or large quantities of objects differed in life from persons buried with little or nothing. That is, larger numbers of goods, rare objects, and better quality items often signify high status. When some young children, for example, were buried with thousands of beads and other artifacts alongside children with no grave objects at all, researchers suspect that although the children were all loved equally, some came from poor families who could not afford the lavish burials of the wealthy.

Yarrow, the Smithsonian collector, uncovered one remarkable burial, almost certainly that of a Chumash chief, when he and his team dug up a Native cemetery near Santa Barbara. Scraping the dirt aside, they saw the remains of a man buried inside a wooden plank canoe—the most costly item any Chumash could possess. Beside the man rested numerous artifacts, including a small stone carving of a canoe and a finely shaped stone drill, which had probably been used to make the holes in the boat's planks so they could be sewn together. A large, finely fashioned stone bowl,

three stone pipes, and other implements had also accompanied this man on his journey to the afterlife. The excavators noted that the burial differed markedly from others, and they assumed the man must have been a chief. Modern archaeologists agree, for we know from early sources that among the Chumash only chiefs and perhaps a few other wealthy people owned plank canoes.

Status differences and perhaps even the inheritance of wealth emerged among Indians of coastal California at least a thousand years ago. That is the age of a burial uncovered during excavations in the 1940s led by Phil Orr, then head of anthropology at the Santa Barbara Museum of Natural History, on Mescalitan Island, which once existed in the middle of Goleta Slough near the present-day Santa Barbara airport. The remains of the deceased male lay on top of a huge scapula, or shoulder blade, of a whale. Artisans had decorated the scapula elaborately with hundreds of inlaid shell beads and ornaments. Other grave offerings included hundreds of additional shell beads, a sandstone bowl mortar with inlaid beads, a large, tubular stone bead with inlaid shell disc beads, three other tubular stone beads, and at least five abalone shell ornaments. Orr had seen no other burial in the Chumash region as visually striking as this one, even though it held fewer beads than some burials elsewhere. The deceased must have been someone greatly respected by his neighbors, and he clearly differed from people of the same time who were buried with few or no grave goods.

Besides lavish burials, other threads of evidence lead researchers to believe that institutionalized inequality existed long ago in coastal California. Remnants of ancient dance houses, for example, imply that high-status leaders performed ceremonies in them, as was the case at the time of European contact.

Concentrations of unusual shell beads and ornaments in archaeological sites hint that some people owned more valuable jewelry than others.

Currently, researchers debate whether marked inequality can be claimed for coastal California Indians earlier than a thousand years ago. Researchers collect more clues every day, whether hidden in the back rooms of museums or in the depressions left where dance houses once stood in Native settlements. I have no doubt that as we study the question further, we will push that date back by centuries, if not millennia.

Figure 11.1. Abalone shell ornaments associated with a headdress that a Chumash ceremonial performer might have worn when dancing the Swordfish dance.

Religions and Rituals of Native Coastal California

eleven

Heather B. Thakar and Lynn H. Gamble

Alerted by the moon's aspect, the *paha*, or ceremonial leader, dispatches his messenger to summon the village. It is time. Time to celebrate, time to feast, time to dance. Time to carry out the rituals that preserve life and honor the dead.

Evocative songs of myth and magic drift through the cool night air. Villagers congregate in silence near the sacred willow-brush enclosure, which has been consecrated anew for the impending ceremony. Singers, accompanied by the rhythmic cadence of turtle shell rattles and the low tones of elderwood flutes, anticipate the arrival of the dancers.

Led by the chief, the dancers advance in rapid succession. Each man wears the erect owl-feather headdress, eagle feather skirt, and full body paint of an initiate. Once within the sanctuary of the enclosure, which has been elaborately decorated with the feathers of sacrificed raptors, the men leap in turn. They twirl like feathers in the wind before an image of the powerful being Chinigchinich. The people fear him and the dangerous animal spirits—rattlesnakes, tarantulas and other spiders, bears, mountain lions, hawks, and eagles—that ruthlessly enforce his moral code. Represented by effigies mounted on wooden stakes near a vibrant yellow, green, blue, red, black, and white sand painting of the world, Chinigchinich confers power, enforces the social order, and chastises those who would violate sacred rituals. Reverent spectators peer over and through the brush walls surrounding the ceremonial ground as the painted bodies of female dancers, led by the chief's wife, arrive in slow procession, swaying

and stamping their feet in rhythm with the songs.

Fueled by daytime feasts, Acjachemen (Juaneno), Tongva, and other Takic-speaking people of southern coastal California once danced this way through the night, enacting sacred rituals to ensure that their sick would be cured and their hungry fed. Their Chinigchinich religion was one of three major religions practiced by coastal peoples before and after the Spaniards arrived. Along the Santa Barbara Channel, north of the Acjachemens' homeland in today's Orange County, Chumash people had their 'antap secret society. Farther north still, above San Francisco Bay, the Kuksu religious society held sway, with its lengthy seclusions in large, earth-covered dance houses accessible only to the initiated few.

The elites who were inducted into one of these three religious organizations assiduously guarded the rituals that bound together their social, political, natural, and supernatural worlds. Members of the societies served as religious and political leaders; they were the early administrators, politicians, and diplomats of California. Without written languages, California Indians relied on rituals and performances, in which they enacted their sacred beliefs through song and dance, to ensure the maintenance of their traditions. By restricting ritual knowledge to select members of society such as chiefs, elders, and shamans, who acquired the secret knowledge through exhaustive initiation ceremonies, the tribe created a human storehouse of information that would otherwise have been lost with each generation.

Figure 11.2. California Indian turtle shell rattle with bone handle. Originally, it was decorated with shell beads appliquéd with asphaltum.

Scholars owe much of what they know about the Takic speakers' Chinigchinich religion to Acjachemen leaders living near the mission of San Juan Capistrano, southeast of Los Angeles in present-day Orange County, and to the Catholic missionary Father Geronimo Boscana. In the early 1800s, when their people began to be decimated by foreign diseases and the social upheaval of the mission period, a few Chinigchinich initiates, all former chiefs and ritualists, sought to preserve their beliefs by confiding in Father Boscana. They allowed him to observe their feasts and accompanying ceremonies, and through him they left a rich, detailed record of Native ritual and performance in southern California.

Boscana commented that the mystery with which the Acjachemen people performed their rites seemed to "perpetuate respect for them" and to preserve the elites' "ascendancy over the people." Public performances and rituals highlighted and reinforced social differences among Acjachemen villagers that persisted well after European contact. Only initiated members of the Chinigchinich secret society, including the chief and powerful elders such as shamans, could enter the willow-brush enclosure, perform dramatic reenactments of sacred oral narratives, intone ceremonial songs, and perform ritual dances. They alone possessed esoteric knowledge and power. They alone linked the sacred and the secular, the religious and the political. By enforcing inviolable secrecy, ritual leaders controlled and united their communities and, by extension, their world.

Today, archaeologists try to understand the development of the elaborate rituals and religious specialization so richly described by Father Boscana and other early observers. Throughout coastal California, ritual and performance once permeated all aspects of village life, much as the sacraments of a modern church guide the lives of the faithful today. Without the luxury of historical documents for times before Spanish colonization, archaeologists must resort to material remains—to objects left behind by people who celebrated sacred rituals hundreds of years ago.

Acjachemen people told early ethnographers that the origins of the Chinigchinich religion lay in the west, on the rocky shores of the southern Channel Islands. And indeed it was on the small island of

San Clemente that archaeologists in the 1980s first became aware of the antiquity of rituals tied to Chinigchinich. On the island's central plateau, Andrew Yatsko and Mark Raab uncovered striking evidence of pre-Columbian ceremonialism that was remarkably consistent with rituals Boscana described, in which Acjachemen people sacrificed birds of prey in remembrance of the dead.

During excavations, Yatsko and Raab discovered the well-preserved skeletons of eight raptors buried in what had been a large, unroofed structure, perhaps similar to the sacred enclosure Father Boscana depicted. Each skeleton represented the sacrifice and careful burial, head down, of a young red-tailed hawk, a peregrine falcon, or, in one case, a raven. A simple sea lion scapula or a few rocks left on top of the grave commemorated the offering. The archaeologists concluded that these raptor burials, along with additional evidence of elaborate rituals at the site, provided strong evidence that an intricate complex of ceremonies of the kind associated with the Chinigchinich religion was well developed on San Clemente Island at least five hundred years ago. Whether or not San Clemente was in fact the place where Chinigchinich beliefs originated, it is clear that historically known Chinigchinich rituals developed from much older practices that left traces in ceremonial sites across San Clemente Island.

Just as we must thank Father Boscana for preserving a written record of Chinigchinich ceremonies, so we must thank the eccentric anthropologist John P. Harrington for writing vivid accounts of another secret religious-political organization, the 'antap society of the Chumash. In the early 1900s, Harrington sought out and relentlessly interrogated the last living speakers of the Chumashan languages and amassed an enormous body of only partly digested information about what had been, before Spanish colonization, a flourishing and complex culture. By patiently wading through a seemingly endless sea of Harrington's unpublished field notes, scholars have recently been able to reconstruct many aspects of Chumash social organization, religious beliefs, world view, and astronomy, all of which were intimately linked with the 'antap society.

Figure 11.3. Whistles made from deer leg bones, from the site of the Chumash village of Muwu at Point Mugu, northwest of Los Angeles.

Wealthy Chumash were invited to join the 'antap at a price. Entry into this elite society was privileged and required substantial monetary donations. Chiefs and other wealthy members of the community paid great sums of shell bead money for their children's initiation, but membership was well worth the cost. Initiation rites served as a formal confirmation of education, not unlike a modern college diploma. Ritual knowledge, power, and wealth were imparted —and restricted—to each elite generation. Most leaders in Chumash society were 'antap (see fig. 10.1). All 'antap were powerful.

Charged with maintaining balance in the universe, the 'antap retained exclusive ownership of ritual objects and the knowledge necessary to perform world-renewing ceremonies, bring rain, and heal the sick. They organized elaborate public ceremonies, complete with dramatic dance performances and plentiful feasts. A diarist with the first Spanish expedition to sail through the Santa Barbara Channel in 1542 remarked on how the Chumash danced endlessly around large plazas as part of their ceremonial life. Dedicated open-air dance grounds, protected by windbreaks of poles and mats, provided a communal forum for important ceremonies. Fernando Librado Kitsepawit, one of Harrington's primary Chumash consultants and a natural storyteller, gave a riveting account of the Swordfish dance: "On each breast the dancer made a loop with a belt going about the body at height of the teats, with blackbird and other black feathers as pretty as they can find.... When the man is dancing you can see only his feather skirt and sticks—[you] cannot see his body. He is like an animal he dances so fast." As the dancer whirled before his audience, his headdress looked like a wheel, spinning in one direction and then another as the dancer gave thanks.

But the 'antap society saved its most important dances and songs for performance not in public but in secret, within a sacred enclosure called a siliyik, meaning "the whole world," screened from the public dance grounds. Accompanied by the low tones of beautifully decorated deer-bone whistles, elderwood flutes, and turtle shell rattles, 'antap members gave voice to ritual songs and breathed myth into life. Aided by proprietary charmstones, delicately carved steatite effigies, aromatic smoke from sacred pipes, and brilliant quartz crystals, they brought rain, averted storms, healed sickness, and punished enemies. The Chumash believed that these rituals, if executed properly, mobilized and controlled both natural forces and supernatural powers. In turn, performance of the rituals demonstrated to everyone how the elites upheld the religious, social, and political order for all Chumash people.

We know from archaeological excavations that 'antap retained their status and ownership of ritual objects even in death. One day in 1926, David Banks Rogers, the first curator of anthropology at the Santa Barbara Museum of Natural History, made an extraordinary discovery while investigating a Chumash archaeological site near Santa Barbara. He had already found some human burials when his eye caught a glint of abalone flashing in the sunlight, and he realized it came from the inlaid skull of a swordfish. Rogers knew immediately that anyone buried with such an exceptional object must have been different from other villagers. He slowly peeled back the earth, revealing what likely was the remains of a Swordfish dancer. Entombed approximately thirteen hundred years ago wearing full ritual regalia, the dancer had entered the next world crowned with an abalone-inlaid skull of the revered swordfish and draped in an ornate cape

Figure 11.4. Replica of a swordfish headdress buried with a man near Santa Barbara, California, thirteen hundred years ago. It consists of a swordfish skull decorated with shell beads and abalone shell ornaments. Chumash dancers wore such headdresses to impersonate the swordfish, a being revered as the chief of all sea animals.

of abalone shell ornaments. Rogers worked at a time when archaeologists had few qualms about excavating ancient cemeteries; today, they try to avoid finding burials at all cost. Yet this discovery still speaks to the remarkable time depth and continuity of Chumash ritual and performances. Passed down from generation to generation through the careful training of initiates, the skills of the Swordfish dancer survived to enthrall Fernando Librado more than a thousand years later.

Farther north along the coast, above San Francisco Bay, the intense initiation rituals of secret societies reached extreme elaboration in the Kuksu religion of the Pomo and Patwin tribes. For the Pomo and Patwin, as for the southern California religious societies to some extent, an impor-tant public role of the Kuksu religion was the initiation and training of boys and girls. Children marked for membership in the Kuksu secret society underwent complex rites and formal instruction that qualified them for elevation to leadership positions. Like Chumash 'antap rituals, Kuksu ceremonies integrated the sacred and the secular, but instead of the 'antap society's single level of membership, the Kuksu society recognized three levels. Hesi initiates became ceremonial spirit dancers, kuksu initiates studied the magic of great curers and shamans, and wai-saltu initiates became mediators between the dead and the living.

Figure 11.5. Headdresses worn by nineteenth-century Pomo Indian dancers, collected in Mendocino County, California. *Left:* flicker-feather headdress worn by a man on the back of the head, secured to a hairnet by the long wooden pin; about eight inches wide. *Right:* woman's fur headdress with red-shafted flicker feathers and quills, glass beads, and cloth; about twelve inches long.

Figure 11.6. A Wintu Indian named Salvador wearing the long feather cloak of a *hesi*, or spirit dancer, in the Kuksu secret society. He is dancing about the pole in front of a dance house.

Power permeated all three levels. As adults, all Kuksu secret society members enjoyed social, economic, and political privileges over nonmembers. The remarkable few who were initiated into all three levels possessed greater supernatural power, esoteric knowledge, and wealth than those initiated into only one. They were the elite of the elite.

Yet an aura of danger permeated *kuksu* and *wai-saltu* initiation ceremonies. Young initiates were isolated in great, smoke-blackened, belowground dance houses, settings designed to enhance the menace and mystery that hung over events within them. In the summer of 1923, an elderly Patwin man named Tony Bill revealed a scar near his navel and divulged the story of his own Kuksu initiation to the ethnographer Alfred Kroeber. The firsthand stories told by Tony Bill and other Patwin men transport us back in time through vivid remembrance. They all go something like this:

Late in the morning, as the sun climbs high, Kuksu, a mythical figure impersonated by a Kuksu society member, leaps from the brush, frightening women as they collect seeds. Painted completely black, his face is unrecognizable. Wearing little more than his black crow-feather headdress, Kuksu clutches a long, sharp, double-edged hairpin and capers through the village. He runs and turns in four circles outside before descending five feet into the great dance house. Inside, he again runs and turns, then sits and lays a small bundle of sticks before the chief, demanding payment for his appearance. The chief urges spectators to deposit shell beads and other small valuables. Kuksu gathers his reward but does not depart. He

Figure 11.7. Archaeological remains of a dance house in California's San Joaquin Valley, probably dating to the early historic period.

returns, frequenting the dance house for three or four days, his job not yet done.

Anticipation builds throughout the community. Everyone knows Kuksu's arrival and performance signal the start of the ritual initiation for "marked" children of wealthy families. Hearing the ritual song that accompanies the initiation ceremony, people gather nearby. Abetted by two associates, known as *limo saltu*, Kuksu seizes prospective initiates. The *limo saltu* hold the captured children, stripped of clothing, over the south roof opening of the dance house. From deep within, Kuksu aims a small, flint-headed arrow at their tender bellies and shoots. Blood flows. Great wails arise as people watch the initiates struggle, get shot, and then be lowered down into the dance house.

Sequestered inside for two to three months, the novices endure a protracted convalescence, isolated from the world outside. Shamans cure them using special medicines. Senior Kuksu society members instruct them in esoteric knowledge. When the time to emerge finally arrives, it happens with great ceremony. Kuksu tosses the neophytes over a fire and then pitches them out of the sacred dance house. Joyful mothers, anxiously waiting above, douse the children in water, returning them to life. Marked in the belly, just like Tony Bill, members of the Kuksu society are permanently joined to one other and to their community, and just as permanently, they become leaders.

To Kuksu initiates, dance houses were home,

hospital, prison, temple, school, and much more. To the unmarked, who were banned from the concealed rites within, dance houses represented mystery and danger and were sharp reminders of the distinction between the initiated and everyone else. Even on rare occasions when the personified Kuksu permitted select spectators to venture into the darkened space, strict seating arrangements reinforced social hierarchies and differential power (plate 13). Carefully constructed and maintained, dance houses physically symbolized central tenets of the Kuksu religion. Indeed, esoteric rituals and performances were so intimately associated with ceremonial dance houses that archaeologists use the presence of such houses to measure the antiquity and geographical extent of the Kuksu religion. Subterranean structures ranging from 90 to 164 feet in diameter in the southern San Joaquin Valley and other parts of central California suggest that Kuksu initiation rituals developed well before historic times.

Why did California Indians spend so much time staging elaborate, carefully executed rituals? One reason was that the celebratory feasting, dancing, and singing brought large groups of people together for social contact and the sharing of food. Single young men and women attending ceremonial events could meet suitable marriage partners from nearby villages. Events aligned with seasonal harvests of acorns, fish, and other essential foods maximized the use of plentiful yields. Ceremonial exchanges of food for bead money, a key element of many ritual occasions, allowed groups whose food supplies had failed that season to share in their neighbors' bounty.

Public ceremonies reinforced the legitimacy of chiefs and other elites, whose authority was manifested in ritual paraphernalia and economic goods. Only the elites, through initiation, could wield the powerful and potentially dangerous forces contained in sacred flutes, turtle shell rattles, feather poles, and other regalia. Young initiates, undoubtedly with mixed feelings, awaited the day when they could sing the sacred songs, handle the impressive paraphernalia, and finally venture into a clandestine world infused with danger and intrigue, a world that would afford them special entitlements and authority in both present life and the life yet to come.

Figure 12.1. A Tolowa woman from the far northern coast of California wearing a long shell bead necklace, probably of clamshell discs made by Pomo Indians, looped many times around her neck. She also wears a buckskin apron covered in shell decorations.

Shell Beads as Adornment and Money

Lynn H. Gamble

The Chumash man paused on the trail. He had walked more than thirty miles, and his load of shelled acorns seemed to have grown ever heavier as he approached the large settlement of Shisholop on the coast. Adjusting the tump band that rested on his forehead and held the heavy basket on his back, he thought about what he might do with the many strands of shell beads he would receive in exchange for his acorns. He might buy some fresh fish and abalones to take back to his home in Piru. There he could contribute to a feast and gain a lot of respect for his generosity.

In Shisholop, the chief of the town, bedecked in strings of shell beads wrapped around his neck and wound on top of his head, emerged from his smoky house to greet the visitor. After the customary exchanges, the two men sat down together. Acorns collected from the coast live oak were a favorite of the chief's, and this trader's stock looked fresh and free of wormholes. The chief removed some strings of beads from his head and showed them to his tired visitor, pointing out their uniformity and the quality of their craftsmanship. They had been made, he said, by one of the best bead makers on Santa Cruz Island. After haggling a bit over the price of the acorns, the two agreed on an amount, and the chief measured out his payment in beads. He wrapped a string of them two and a half times around his hand, from the end of his middle finger to his wrist, and then repeated the motion several times, almost as if by sleight of hand, until the correct amount was laid out.

My fictional chief and acorn trader did not spring unfounded from my imagination. Historical records and archaeological finds show that exchanges much like this one took place all over Native California, long before Spaniards arrived and for decades afterward. Pomo Indians living north of San Francisco Bay, for example, scheduled seasonal feasts at which people exchanged beads for food. During the fall, when Pomo groups living in the foothills gathered more acorns than they could eat or store, they planned a feast to which they invited people living along the creeks and lakes. The guests arrived laden with shell beads, which their chiefs presented to the host chief. After several days of feasting, sweat bathing, gambling, and visiting, the host chief calculated how many acorns his group would provide in return for the beads and gave them to the guests. Months later, when fish were in overabundance, the roles switched. Chiefs living on creeks and other waterways sent out invitations to acorn collectors, who came to feast and exchange beads for fish. In this way, Pomo people who lived in different habitats shared their harvests, using beads as the medium of exchange.

Traded far and wide, shell beads turn up in archaeological sites all over California. Besides exchanging them for food, people used them as objects of decoration and adornment continuously for at least eight thousand years, making them one of the longest-running forms of California Indian material culture. Artisans fashioned other raw materials, such as stone and bone, into beads as well, but no material was as ubiquitous as shell.

California Indians created beads from the shells

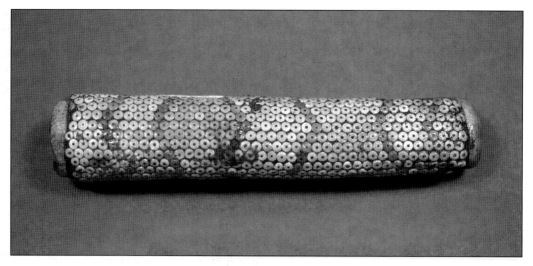

Figure 12.2. Deer bone tube, almost six inches long, with appliquéd shell beads, from an archaeological site in Santa Barbara called Burton Mound.

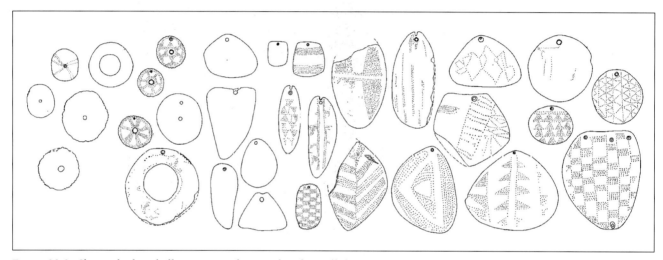

Figure 12.3. Chumash clamshell ornaments decorated with small depressions drilled to create a design.

of more than twenty-two species of sea animals, including abalone, clam, purple olive (of the genus *Olivella*), and tooth shell (genus *Dentalium*). Shells of the different species vary in color, and craftspeople strung them together to create multihued necklaces, bracelets, and belts. The outer portions of red abalone shells, for example, are reddish brown, while those of the so-called black abalone are dark green. Beads cut from mussel shells were blue or bluish black, sometimes with a yellowish hue. Often these colored beads were strung with whitish or grayish purple beads made from olive shells, creating striking contrasts. During some time periods, Chumash Indians preferred to wear conspicuous jewelry that could be seen

readily from a distance. One example is the large deer bone bead shown in figure 12.2, which has blue mussel, red abalone, and white *Olivella* beads appliquéd onto it with asphaltum in a chevron pattern. Showy ornaments like this one might have served as badges signifying social position.

About eight hundred years ago the Chumash and other tribes began to recognize certain kinds of beads as money. They crafted these beads, which would pass from hand to hand many times over, using the thickest portion of the olive shell, which was harder to drill and more durable than the thinner wall portions. Chumash islanders specialized in bead making, partly because they wanted products

Figure 12.4. Small mussel-shell disc beads from an archaeological site in Thousand Oaks, California. Most measure just under one-sixteenth inch in diameter.

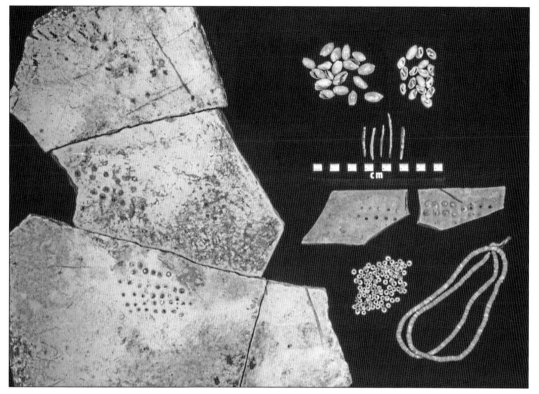

Figure 12.5. A Chumash bead-making kit, with olive shells and beads in different stages of manufacture, stone drills (*center right*), and sandstone slabs on which beads were drilled and ground. The drill on the right is about one and one-half inches long.

from the mainland and needed valuable goods of their own to exchange for them. Early historical accounts describe how Chumash islanders traded beads for things such as desirable seeds, fox skin shawls, and feather headdresses made by Chumash living in the interior, as well as for services. The exchange of beads for goods and services allowed the Chumash to create widespread networks of people associated with one another not only for trade but also for social purposes such as finding wives and husbands. Mission records document many marriages between Chumash islanders and mainlanders.

Nowhere in California is evidence of bead making as abundant as it is on the northern Santa Barbara Channel Islands. Small, broken stone drills that once made the holes in beads, partially drilled shell beads split in half, and shell detritus all attest to bead manufacture on the islands. At some archaeological sites, thousands of broken olive shells litter the surface. Remains of bead making are so profuse on Santa Cruz Island that it became known as the "original mint." In some settlements on Santa Cruz, most households made beads, some of which are so small they can easily slip through mesh as fine as a window screen.

When photographing the tiny beads shown in figure 12.4, I had to hold my hold breath so that they did not roll about.

It was a tedious occupation, bead making. First the artisan searched a sandy beach for olive shells, a favored material partly because it was so durable. Yet its hardness also made it difficult to work. Laboriously, the bead maker broke open the shells and chipped the pieces into roughly shaped discs. With enough of these finally on hand, he or she spent many more hours drilling them, stringing them, and then grinding their edges smooth against a stone anvil.

That people drilled such small beads using only stone tools is almost inconceivable. Chester King, one of the foremost scholars of shell beads, was the first to document the specialized activity of making chert stone bead drills on Santa Cruz Island. For years he studied collections in the back rooms of museums, documenting changes over time in the styles and materials of beads and in the drills used for perforating them. In the summer of 1967, at a site on Santa Cruz Island dating to sometime in the last eight hundred years, King discovered hundreds of chert "cores," pieces of stone from which Chumash people had knapped small blades that became drills. Clearly, the residents of this village had specialized in producing drills, which they traded to other villages, especially on the western end of the island, where people specialized in making beads for use as money.

Both before and after California Indians began to use shell beads as currency, they took hundreds of thousands of them out of circulation over the centuries by burying them with the dead. Doing so not only met ritual needs but also helped maintain a constant market for more beads. Archaeologists have gained much of their knowledge of shell beads and ornaments by studying artifacts collected as parts of burials in times when graves were still excavated, a practice most archaeologists avoid today. One of the most spectacular examples is a mass of approximately thirty thousand saucer-shaped olive shell beads uncovered with the burial of a thirty-year-old man at an archaeological site east of San Francisco Bay. Dating to about fifteen hundred years ago, this is the largest documented bead lot found in California so far.

This collection of beads testifies both to the deceased's wealth and status and to the far-flung extent of trade among California Indians. Multiple lines of evidence, including sourcing of the raw materials through isotopic analysis, show that the beads in this man's grave were probably produced in the Santa Barbara Channel region and traded several hundred miles north to the Bay Area. This collection also demonstrates how the popularity of bead styles and perhaps the efficacy of trade networks could change swiftly. The saucer-shaped beads accompanying this burial enjoyed popularity in central California for hundreds of years, but soon after this man died, people stopped burying saucer beads with the dead around San Francisco Bay. Instead, another style of olive shell beads began to appear in graves—a type not found in the Santa Barbara Channel region but believed to have been made locally in the Bay Area. We do not know whether the new style simply became locally fashionable or whether something happened to disrupt trade routes between north and south, but this sort of pattern is typical throughout the state. The popularity of different bead types and raw materials waxed and waned continuously over the millennia.

The trade in beads between the Santa Barbara Channel and San Francisco Bay areas was itself typical for California. Traders spread shell beads, many of them Chumash made, all over the state and indeed over much of western North America. At even greater distances, excavators have discovered Chumash beads in archaeological sites as far east as Pecos Pueblo, New Mexico, and as far north as the Columbia River.

The meanings and value of beads shifted as they passed through networks of people. In some places they served as currency with economic value; in others, as political symbols; and in still others, as objects denoting status. For example, among the Cahuilla, who live today in the Colorado Desert of southern California, around the modern town of Palm Springs, shell beads that had been produced as money in the Channel Islands took on a different meaning. Cahuilla people associated them primarily with ceremonies, and they were owned not by individuals but by the clan. Anyone traveling through Cahuilla country could identify the clan leader by the distinctive tattoos on his forearms, which he used to measure out strings of beads.

The energy California Indians expended in producing millions of shell beads and ornaments over several thousand years is almost unimaginable. Shell beads were once important in many other places around the world as well, but the labor California Indians invested in them probably exceeded that of any other hunter-gatherers worldwide. Traveling along trade and social networks in California and beyond, shell beads and ornaments connected people who spoke many languages and lived thousands of miles apart into a web of vital relationships.

Figure 13.1. A section of the great panel at Painted Rock before the onset of heavy vandalism.

Chumash Paintings on Stone

William Hyder and Georgia Lee

Intrigued by descriptions of a place called Painted Rock, where Chumash Indians long ago created spectacular designs on a great rock outcrop, we set out early one morning in the late 1970s for the Carrizo Plain, a large, empty valley on maps of the day. Far from the rush of teeming highways, we turned onto a dirt road over which other tourists had made the same trek in the preceding hundred years, first by horse and wagon and later in Model Ts. Some of them, like us, no doubt were drawn by a fanciful tale of shamans and human sacrifice supposedly depicted on the rock, a tale published by Myron Angel in his 1910 book *La Piedra Pintada: The Painted Rock*. We knew the place the instant we saw it: no one could mistake the distinctive horseshoe shape rising from a distant wheat field.

Unsure about proper etiquette and with no sign

Figure 13.2. Painted Rock, a unique sandstone formation on California's Carrizo Plain.

of life in the nearby dilapidated farmhouse, we parked our car and began the long hike following a two-track that ran alongside the fields. The rock dwarfed us as we neared its opening, but the paintings drew us deeper into its natural amphitheater. On the left, a painted spider web followed by a fantastic array of figures from Chumash mythology—a turtle, a coyote, a bear, a line of dancers, what appeared to be a human inside a bear, a rattlesnake, a lizard, and fanciful figures too abstract to recognize—appeared in turn, albeit broken and marred by hundreds of carved names and other abuses rendered by unthinking tourists over the years.

As we slowly examined the painted walls and amazing figures, Angel's legend seemed inadequate to explain the complex imagery. Over the coming years we would develop our own stories to try to explain Painted Rock, but not before experiencing close encounters with golden eagles, tarantulas, horned owls, and countless rattlesnakes more surprised by our presence than we were by theirs.

The Chumash were hardly alone among coastal and inland California Indians in making what we now call rock art, whether painted images (pictographs) or carvings (petroglyphs). Tribes painted or carved images that were important to them and that reflected their world view, so the motifs and methods of making them varied from one tribal area to another. Some groups carved or pecked designs on rocks; some, like the Chumash, painted in caves and beneath sheltering overhangs; some made "ground figures" by moving rocks to form a pattern. Each group had its distinctive repertoire of images. Some figures were associated with attempts to control the weather or ensure fertility. In some places, people made designs to bring luck in hunting or fishing.

We have visited, studied, and documented rock carvings and paintings in most parts of California, but we were particularly drawn to the rock art of the Chumash Indians because it is so visually stunning. Rather than consisting of relatively simple patterns or images of animals and people, the often large, elaborate Chumash designs appear to have been generated in people's psyches, perhaps under the influence of fasting or of datura, a hallucinogenic plant also known as jimsonweed. Chumash painters often executed their designs with meticulous detail and fine-line precision. Their images may appear in outline or as a shape outlined with another color, with tiny dots, or with both. Often the paintings are done in monochrome red or in red with black and white (plate 9). An occasional painting includes some yellow, and blue and green appear at a few sites.

Rock art is still important to Native people of California because it is one of the few expressions of their pre-Columbian culture that survives in place today and can be experienced on the spot where it was created. The designs represent elements of people's religion, cosmology, history, and ethnicity, although we often lack the tools necessary to read the messages embodied in their symbolism. The enigma posed by pre-Columbian art invites amateur speculation, artistic interpretation, and sometimes fierce scholarly debates with uncertain conclusions.

As we began studying Painted Rock, we were content at first to photograph and draw the spectacular paintings while ignoring the damage inflicted by gunshots and graffiti. Concerned that more might be lost before anyone acted to preserve the site, Georgia Lee organized a research team of volunteers, anthropologists, archaeologists, and artists, sponsored by the University of California, Berkeley, to draw the surviving paintings to scale and document each instance of graffiti and environmental damage. Thanks to the careful recording, we began to see patterns in the images. Some of them seemed to suggest stories—if we only knew how to read them.

Chumash oral narratives written down by the ethnographer and linguist John P. Harrington in the early

SLO 79 Locus 1:19 ▨ Red ▨ Black

Figure 13.3. Coyote and lizard panel at Painted Rock.

1900s led us to an unexpected breakthrough in our attempts to make sense of the rock paintings. Literal readings of recorded myths explained that coyotes have long snouts because they spent so much time calling *tsu-tsu*, stretching their lips in search of a sweet kiss from the young girls. Coyote declared that people should have fine hands like his, but lizard waited in silence and darted forward at the last minute to give humans hands shaped like his, much to coyote's dismay. There on the wall of Painted Rock were coyote with his long snout and lizard with his foot superimposed on coyote's paw. Was it possible that we could actually know what the long-dead artists wanted to say with their art?

Renewed intellectual and public interest in rock art exploded when it became apparent that ethnographies might provide clues to the meanings behind the art. Harrington extracted stories and legends from elderly Chumash informants, some of them on their deathbeds. When his notes became available to scholars in the late 1960s and early 1970s, they opened new windows into Chumash culture. Whether this renewed interest led to better understandings or merely created more confusion is debatable, but it did

Figure 13.4. Distinctive mandala- and sunlike paintings at Painted Cave. These designs have inspired interpretations based on ethnographic descriptions of Chumash astronomy.

spur efforts to find and study sites that had long been protected by their remote locations and anonymity. By 1985, hiking guides included directions to the best-known sites, and many of them could be found simply by following the newly worn paths leading to them. Places such as Pool Rock, in Los Padres National Forest, were so damaged by weekend sightseers that the area had to be closed to unregulated visits (plate 18).

Something similar had happened a century earlier, in the 1880s, to a Chumash rock art site in the hills above Santa Barbara, a site called Painted Cave. Its paintings captured the urban public's imagination after a nearby resort opened the cave for visits. Painted Cave's popularity threatened its survival as visitors began carving their names and initials into the paintings. In order to protect them, the owners installed an iron grill said to have come from a Santa Barbara bank

vault. That same grill protects the well-known and publicly accessible cave to this day.

The images at Painted Cave can inspire viewers to move beyond the literal interpretations evoked by Chumash myths. Someone leaning against the back wall of Painted Cave, looking outward, experiences a very different perspective from that of a tourist standing outside the grill, looking in. Now the paintings' fantastic circular, sun-wheel, and mandala-like designs seem to float around the viewer's head. They strongly resemble rock art from other parts of the world known to have been painted by people under the effects of hallucinogenic drugs. And indeed, both Chumash men and women sometimes took datura, and shamans often used it to increase their power. Chumash people in datura-induced hallucinogenic states are known to have painted images that correspond closely to the designs in Painted Cave,

Figure 13.5. Sunlight interacting with circular painted images at Bear Paw Cave. Such interactions are often interpreted as evidence for Chumash astronomy and related activities of Chumash shamans.

particularly in the tiny white dots outlining some images.

Another visitor to Painted Cave saw something quite different. A black circle surrounded by tiny white dots appeared to be the sun in full eclipse, and the many circular elements seemed to be the brightest stars, which would have become visible in the temporary darkness. Could it be that the popular interpretation—that of shamans painting images they saw during hallucinations—was clouded by preconceptions, and the paintings were really the work of Chumash astronomers?

We could not re-create a solar eclipse to compare the sky with the Painted Cave mural, but we were able to examine another Chumash rock art site purported to feature an astronomical marker. We had visited Condor Cave on several occasions and noted an enigmatic hole carved through one wall, which other researchers had claimed was a marker of the sun's rise on the winter solstice. If we could witness sunrise at Condor Cave on that day, we would learn

whether or not the sun actually shone through the hole. Our anticipation built as we set out to trek into the Santa Barbara backcountry on a moonless, nearly pitch-black night. Given what we had heard about the site, we imagined a brilliant beam of light piercing the cave's interior as the sun broke over the distant ridge.

Our hike ended in the subdued light of early morning, not yet daybreak but bright enough to make walking easy. By the time we reached the cave, the light was too bright for a beam to be visible, even though the sun had not yet cleared the ridge. We could see the sunrise through the hole, but we realized that the event would be replicated every day for a month or two on either side of the solstice. Nothing remarkable happened inside the cave, leading us to believe that earlier descriptions had been heavily romanticized.

Despite our disappointment, we do not fully discount the possibility that some sites contain celestial imagery. A painting of concentric circles at a site known as Bear Paw Cave is highlighted by

Figure 13.6. Bear paw petroglyph pecked in the shelter wall at Pool Rock.

the sun's light and shadow in interesting ways. The painting might have been deliberately placed to create interaction with the sun, although the effects are not restricted to a solstice or other ceremonial time. Chumash shamans were known to have used wands called sun sticks during winter solstice ceremonies to "pull the sun back on track." Surviving sun sticks in museum collections are topped with stone discs painted with designs like those found on cave walls. A small, barely visible painting on the wall of Condor Cave appears to be an example of a shaman with a sun stick. Proving or refuting explanations for rock art imagery is never easy.

Our solstice hike was not a total disappointment. We saw fresh bear tracks along the trail, not unlike the pecked bear tracks found beneath the condor painting that gives the cave its name (plate 21). The Chumash shared their environment with bears and often competed with them for the same foods. We would have been surprised not to have found bear imagery in their

rock art. One Chumash story recounts the fate of an elderly bear shaman. Feeling that his time was near, the old man walked off into the hills and disappeared. A friend, worried about his fate, followed his tracks until the human footprints became bear tracks and then disappeared. Bear track images and bears themselves are ubiquitous throughout Chumash territory.

Harrington recorded stories about Chumash shamans, although only a few mention their direct involvement in making rock art. One story tells how a malevolent shaman created a rock painting in order to cause a famine. He was said to have painted on a stone several figures of men and women falling down and bleeding from the mouth. He took the rock into the hills while making prayers for sickness. His efforts were rewarded by a great drought that caused many deaths, but other shamans found out about the painting and threw the stone into a body of water. It then began to rain.

A few small painted stones have been found in springs in Chumash country in the way mentioned in this story, lending credence to the tale. Freshwater springs figure prominently in Chumash stories, and healing rituals often took place at springs. Aquatic themes figure prominently in the paintings at many sites; we can recognize salamanders, water striders, frogs, and a curved figure with bifurcated ends that is often called an "aquatic figure." Several such elements fill a natural cavity outlined with an arrowhead-shaped calcium deposit at a site known as Arrowhead Springs, high in the Santa Ynez Mountains, with spectacular vistas of the Santa Barbara Channel and the villages that lined the coast.

Modern patterns of landownership require visitors to approach Arrowhead Springs from the top of the mountain, but Chumash people would have trekked up from the coast. Most likely, the prehistoric trail passed other painting sites and isolated images painted on boulders. Perhaps the artists made the climb to gather acorns or other foodstuffs (mortars are found nearby), but it would have been a hard trip for little gain. We believe they visited the spring as a destination in its own right, to perform rituals there.

We have found the spring at Arrowhead Springs active on even the hottest days of the driest years. One image painted on the calcium deposit, a fish with human arms, leaves little doubt that the place is special. The figure holds a wand with a pinwheel top in one hand, and an accompanying arrowhead-shaped headdress mimics the shape of the calcium deposit. The water-themed paintings and unusual natural calcium accretion make it difficult to believe the site could be anything but a sacred shrine like those documented in Chumash ethnography.

A small rock overhang near the head of a coastal canyon on Vandenberg Air Force Base protects a vivid naturalistic painting of a swordfish, which calls to mind a different story about the importance of the sea in Chumash art and ritual. The Chumash hunted swordfish on the open sea, and the creature figures prominently in many myths. In the 1920s, at an old Chumash cemetery near Santa Barbara, David Banks Rogers excavated a burial containing a swordfish headdress along with a sparkling, iridescent, abalone shell cape (chapter 11). Tehachapi George, a Chumash descendant, identified it as the regalia of a Swordfish dancer, someone who performed in honor of the swordfish, who "brought the Chumash whale meat in plenty."

We believe the case is strong that shamans created at least some Chumash rock art. The symbolism certainly meets our expectations for hallucinogenic imagery   brilliant sunlike images, fantastic creatures, indescribable abstractions—whether it was triggered by psychoactive drugs or self-induced trance. With few exceptions, the images appear to have been painted by a practiced artist or technician, so the act of painting seems to have been restricted to a small number of specialists.

Although most Chumash imagery seems to consist of abstractions related to religious activities, artists depicted significant or extraordinary events as well. In a small valley in the Santa Monica Mountains, someone painted on a protected wall of a large volcanic outcrop what might be a record of the first Spanish overland trek into southern California. Four equestrians, painted in red, cross a panel of figures with human features, many of which appear to be birds or figures wearing elaborate headdresses. These figures may represent leaders dressed to greet the foreign visitors. The ritual leaders of Chumash society, the 'antap, often wore elaborate costumes of feathers and animal skins for ceremonial dances. A more elaborate painting at Burro Flats, in the same area, portrays a possible feathered dancer in greater detail (plate 19).

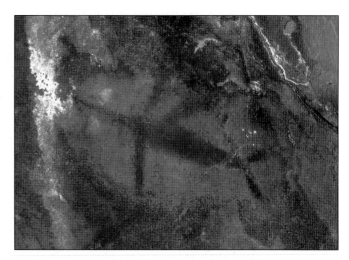

Figure 13.7. Naturalistic painting of a swordfish that inspired the name Swordfish Cave.

The sea played an important role in the creation stories of all Native peoples of coastal California. The Chumash, who journeyed to the Channel Islands in plank canoes, likely imbued aquatic symbols with special significance, if not spiritual power. Incised ships found at coastal rock art sites and on mission walls demonstrate the reverence the Chumash continued to hold well into historic times for those who mastered the sea. An incised sailing ship at a coastal site known as Rattlesnake Shelter, on Vandenberg Air Force Base, was probably carved by a Chumash *vaquero* tending sheep sometime after 1850. The ship *Yankee Blade* ran aground in 1854 not far from Rattlesnake Shelter. Whether the incised figure is the *Yankee Blade* or another sailing ship of the period, Chumash ranch hands continued to create documentary forms of rock art after California became a state.

Our efforts to document and understand Chumash rock art have led us from identifying images drawn from mythology and cosmology to recognizing Chumash people's complex understanding of the heavens. Further still, we have come to appreciate the role of shamans and other political and religious leaders in maintaining cultural stability and explaining their rapidly changing world at the point of Spanish contact. Yet no matter how certain we feel about our understanding of many of the images, we are equally certain that the artistic expressions of the Native peoples of coastal California will continue to invite interpretation.

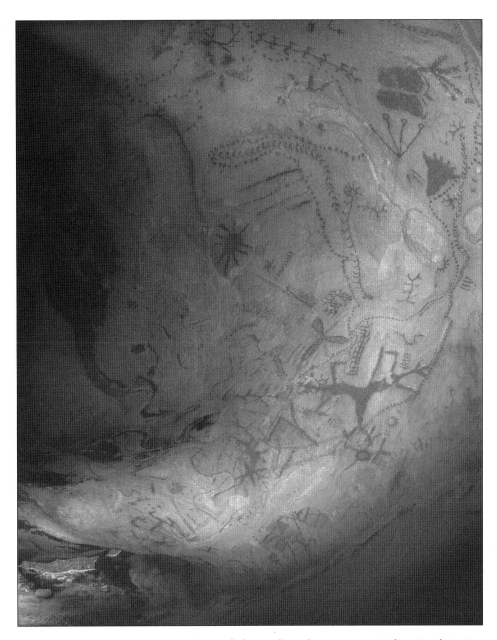

Figure 13.8. Intricate paintings on the roof of a small sandstone cave on Indian Creek, in Los Padres National Forest. They are perhaps a stylized depiction of the Milky Way.

Figure 14.1. Indian dancers participating in a celebration in the plaza of Mission San Francisco. Lithographic reproduction of an 1816 painting by Louis Choris.

Colonization's Cultural Earthquake

Julia G. Costello and John R. Johnson

When first confronted by the European world, California Indians interpreted their encounters in supernatural terms. In 1916 an Inseño Chumash woman named María Solares told the anthropologist John P. Harrington that "when the first whites came here, the [Indians]…said 'it is not people, it is of the other world.'" She went on: "Long ago an ox got loose from [a Spanish herd] and wandered up country here and suddenly came on the inhabitants of Kalawashaq [a village, or *ranchería*].… They went to [the ox] and put *shoxsh* [an offering of feathered down] on it and did not know what it was."

Native Californians' long-established ways of life would be forever altered by developments on continents thousands of miles away, where European nations pursued unprecedented economic and political expansion. Advances in shipbuilding and navigation and an insatiable demand for new sources of materials and goods fueled this global reach. Following Columbus's arrival in the Caribbean in 1492, Spain spread its royal cloak over much of the American continents. In the next century, expeditions sailed the California coast and claimed it for the Crown. Fragments of brightly decorated porcelain and heavy pieces of iron excavated from village sites north of San Francisco signal some of the earliest contacts between Native Californians and Europeans. The Coast Miwok people who lived there, marveling over their new acquisitions, could not have anticipated the cataclysmic and irreversible changes they heralded.

Spain launched its campaign to settle California in 1769, to ward off competition from the north by Russians and the British. They employed three institutions: the presidio, or military fort; the mission, where Franciscan priests taught Spanish culture to Native people; and the *pueblo*, where the civilian population lived. San Diego, in 1769, and Monterey, in 1770, received the first pairs of presidios and missions. Over the next fifty-three years, nineteen additional missions, two presidios, and three pueblos joined those initial establishments.

The Franciscan Junípero Serra served as California's "father president" during the colony's formative years, founding the first nine missions. He chose locations favored by the presence of numerous Indians, available water, and plentiful agricultural land. Early Indian recruits to the missions were taught to build structures of pole and thatch, which they eventually replaced with more substantial buildings of adobe and stone as they acquired new building skills.

Spain found conquering and converting the California Natives to be challenging. In Mexico and South America, the colonizers had met organized military empires with centralized governments, such as those of the Aztecs and Incas. Victory in a few big military battles sufficed to subjugate local populations, because the Spaniards themselves simply replaced the previous ruling elites. In California they had to negotiate with the chiefs of every small, autonomous tribe to win their tolerance for the founding of each mission and presidio. Success with one group did not ensure acceptance by its neighbors, and some missions struggled for security for decades, in conflict with Indians whose land they had taken.

It is fair to ask why Native people not only largely tolerated the Spanish invasion but even, to some extent, became willing participants in the imposed culture. One factor—also key to the rapid spread of industrialized societies worldwide—was the compelling attraction of the new and exotic. Spaniards introduced into California a cornucopia of enticements: cattle and horses, incense and candles, wheat and corn, guitars and trumpets, mirrors and bells, silk and iron, even fireworks from China. Buildings made of earth rose from the ground, and water turned from its course caused the ground to bloom. As individuals and families were drawn to the Spaniards' apparent centers of magic and power, old village systems became destabilized. Traditional religious rituals could not prevent rampant deaths from new diseases, the destruction of food plants by introduced livestock, and the disruption of traditional trading alliances. Demoralized and confused, Native villagers increasingly surrendered to the new life offered at the missions.

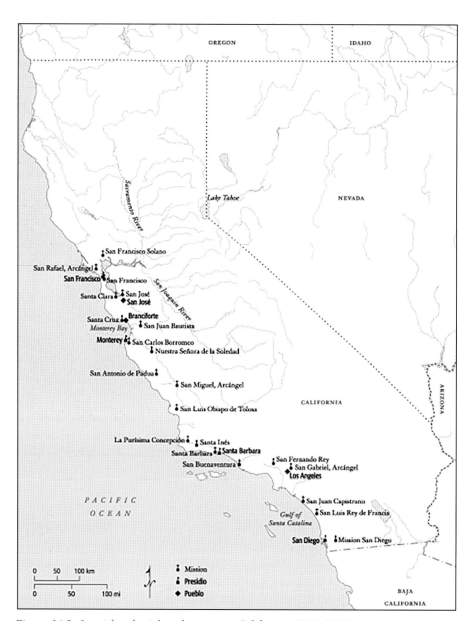

Figure 14.2. Spanish colonial settlements in California, 1769–1822.

There, Native populations reached, on average, a thousand persons, although some missions exceeded three thousand residents. Two Franciscan priests administered each mission complex, supported by seven to ten military guards provided by the district presidio. A preference for married soldiers with families reduced unwanted relations between Spanish men and Native women. Self-sufficient complexes, missions were laid out with a common plan. San Diego resident José Bandini, in his *A Description of California in 1828*, described the mission *casco*, or central headquarters: "The buildings in some of the missions are more extensive than in others, but they are almost alike in form.... In all of them are comfortable living quarters for the ministers, warehouses for the storing of goods, granaries large enough for the grain, places for making soap, rooms of weaving, carpenter shops, forges, wine presses, cellars, large patios and corrals, separate apartments for the Indian youth of both sexes, and, finally, as many workrooms as the establishment may require. Adjoining these and connected with them are the churches."

Also located at the casco were the Indian village, quarters for soldiers and their families, walled gardens and orchards, reservoirs and washing areas, and industrial facilities such as mills and kilns.

Figure 14.3. The *casco* of old Mission La Purísima, which was destroyed by earthquake in 1812. This artist's reconstruction is based on studies by archaeologists, historians, and architectural historians. The Indian village is on the left, soldiers' quarters are on the right, and gardens are to the rear.

Surrounding this core of activity, far-reaching territory encompassed fields and gardens where workers grew specialty crops such as grapes and summer wheat. There were outlying ranches with their own permanent buildings and resident populations; grazing land for cattle, sheep, and horses; stone quarries; and monumental water systems with dams, ditches, and aqueducts.

Once baptized, Indians became "neophytes"— permanent members of the mission community, subject to European social customs—and received education in useful vocations. A neophyte lived with a foot in each of two worlds, continuing traditional Native practices while using new Spanish skills. Archaeology in neophyte residences reveals families residing in both adobe buildings and brush dwellings, cooking over fire rings, fashioning stone tools, harvesting local foods, and practicing traditional ceremonies. Many mission Indians maintained social and political alliances carried over from their home villages, even while developing new social networks

around meals, gambling, work, and celebrations. Some skilled neophytes could hire themselves out to nearby presidios and pueblos. José Francisco Ortega, commander of the Santa Barbara presidio, complained that he would be able to complete its construction considerably faster "if only he could get enough glass beads" to pay local Chumash workers in a form of currency they valued.

California Indian tribes suffered profoundly from this cultural upheaval. In a process called *reducción*, implemented in all but the southernmost missions of California, baptized Indians moved from their traditional villages to the mission casco. As missions expanded, they drew converts from more distant regions and gathered Native groups speaking different languages—often established enemies—into large communities where they were expected to live peacefully.

Enforced schedules of work and prayer could be oppressive to people accustomed to responding to seasonal demands. The padres typically characterized

Figure 14.4. Chumash necklace composed of glass trade beads and Native-made tubular beads from the purple-hued hinge of the giant rock scallop. Indian women at Mission Santa Inés wore necklaces like this one.

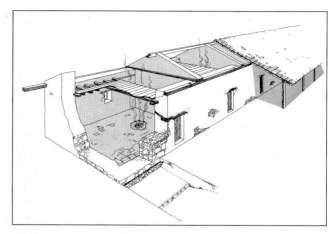

Figure 14.5. Rooms of Indian families at Mission Santa Cruz, reconstructed after archaeological excavations of the adobe building.

neophytes who met onerous work regimes with passive resistance as "indolent" or "ignorant." Chronic discord also arose from the padres' insistence on modesty, chastity, and monogamous, life-long marriages, which ran counter to many traditional practices. Punishment for disobedience often included public lashings, a practice that, although common in Europe, appalled Native people. Mission Indians sometimes resisted these rules overtly (chapter 15). The Chumash uprising of 1824 was a spectacular instance of coordinated rebellion involving the populations of Missions Santa Inés, La Purísima, and Santa Barbara. The murder and mutilation of Fray Andrés Quintana at Mission Santa Cruz dramatically avenged his reported use of an iron-tipped horsewhip for punishments.

It is difficult to generalize about conditions at the California missions, which varied considerably in economic productivity, relations with Native groups, and circumstances of daily life. A visitor in the 1830s reported that some missions' buildings "are tiled and whitewashed and look neat and comfortable; others are dirty and in disrepair and in every way uncomfortable." Although economic success depended heavily on local climate and land productivity, it was the personalities of the padres that established the tenor of mission life. Resident fathers remained at their institutions for decades and held nearly autonomous power. When the American trader Alfred Robinson visited California in 1829, he remarked that although most mission padres were charitable and responsible, some were not. He strongly criticized a priest at San

Fernando whose ugly character was reflected in both his management of the mission and the misery of its inhabitants.

The conditions of mission life, including the practice of reducción, had other devastating consequences. From their earliest years, most of the California missions suffered catastrophic death rates. Densely populated Indian villages at the missions enabled rapid transmission of diseases, promoting the spread of imported Spanish maladies to which the Indians had no resistance. Measles, influenza, and typhoid raced through the villages. Rampant syphilis, introduced by presidio soldiers, caused long and tragic illnesses. The new pathogens devastated the most vulnerable segments of the population—women of childbearing age, newborn infants, and young children—so that the population declined drastically in each succeeding generation.

In response to these losses, established missions reached farther into the interior to replace their shrinking populations. Toward the end of his life, Father President Mariano Payeras, in a letter written from Mission La Purísima in February 1820, lamented that because of disease, he and his Franciscan brothers had perhaps brought more harm than good to the Native peoples of California: "It pains and saddens our Christian hearts exceedingly because where we expected a beautiful and flourishing church and some beautiful towns which would be the joy of the sovereign majesties of heaven and earth, we find ourselves with…a people miserable and sick, with

Figure 14.6. Archaeological excavations at Mission San Buenaventura, 2011, exposing an original tile floor in the east quadrangle. In the photograph is Julie Tumamait-Stenslie, a descendant of the Ventureño Chumash Indians who lived at the mission.

rapid depopulation of rancherías which with profound horror fills the cemeteries."

In view of such mortality and mistreatment, it is fair to question why many Indians stayed at the missions. The traveler Georg Heinrich von Langsdorff pondered this dilemma when he observed in 1806 that "two or three monks, and four or five soldiers, keep in order a community of a thousand or fifteen hundred rough uncivilized men, making them lead a wholly different course of life from that to which they had been accustomed, without any spirit of mutiny or insurrection." With the colonized vastly outnumbering the colonizers, physical coercion cannot be the only answer. Scholars have postulated that tribes reached a "tipping point" beyond which those left behind in the villages could no longer sustain traditional ways, so that they eventually followed friends and relatives to

the mission communities. Leaving the mission would also have meant abandoning all of one's surviving family and social networks. In general, little remained at former villages: key resources were gone, including wild plants overgrazed by livestock.

Even as the missions struggled to establish themselves, global events foreshadowed great changes in California. Revolts by Spain's New World colonies in the early nineteenth century cut off supply ships to California, and communications from Spanish authorities virtually ceased. Although the California colony voiced allegiance to Spain, its residents trafficked with Yankee and British smugglers who illegally plied the coast and traded vital and luxury goods for cattle hides and tallow from the missions. Archaeologists find evidence for this open market in a sudden increase in fragments of decorated English ceramics and European wine and brandy bottles.

When Mexico won its independence from Spain in 1821, the missions' fate was inevitable. Having thrown off the yoke of royal oppression, newly freed citizens of Mexico demanded access to the vast landholdings of the Catholic Church. All the missions of California were dismantled following the Emancipation and Secularization Decree of 1834. Within a decade, some ten million acres of mission land passed into private ownership, and nearly fifteen thousand Indians gained their freedom. At each institution, all material holdings—land, livestock, orchards, buildings, and furnishings—came under the management of a commissioner appointed by the Mexican provincial governor in Monterey. The commissioners were generally corrupt and self-serving, and most missions fell quickly into disarray. Looking for immediate personal gain, commissioners slaughtered livestock for sale, neglected fields and orchards, stripped missions of building materials, and abandoned vital irrigation systems.

Regulations stipulated that mission land be allotted first to former neophytes and then to soldiers and citizens who had provided service to the colony. In reality, Native people received precious little during this massive giveaway of land to the *gente de razón*, or "people of reason," a term used for non-Natives. Rancho grants, which numbered only thirty before 1834, exploded to more than eight hundred between 1835 and 1847. Most Indians who obtained allotments soon sold out for needed cash or eventually lost them to scheming neighbors. Some neophytes remained in settlements around the old cascos, many others hired out to the new ranchos, working largely for food and lodging, and still others disappeared into the interior. Many second- and third-generation neophytes, who often had skills needed by the burgeoning new state of

Figure 14.7. An Indian family that remained living at Mission San Juan Capistrano after secularization, helping to form the beginnings of the modern town.

California, simply melted into Hispanic communities.

Fortunately, one remnant of the California missions was preserved in archives in California, Mexico, and Spain. Consummate bureaucrats, officials of the Catholic Church left invaluable records of each person's birth, baptism, marriages, and death, often including traditional personal names and village of origin. The documents allow scholars to reconstruct the locations of Native villages, identify social ties between families, and track political alliances between tribal groups. Rarely is such detailed information available for scholars of Native contact with Europeans.

In the case of California, other kinds of documents augment the personal data on individual Indians. Annual reports sent to Spain by both the Catholic clergy and government officials complain candidly about mistreatment of Indians at the hands of soldiers and lament the lack of trained artisans, religious vestments, and even chocolate. They tell of crops planted and harvested, buildings completed, and natural disasters survived. Diaries of foreign expeditions provide independent descriptions of conditions at missions, as well as often insightful accounts of traditional Indian activities. Requisition and shipping lists and manifests of smuggling ships offer additional details of economic life in Spanish and Mexican California. In early years, for example, otter pelts were the most valuable export from the colony. Hunted nearly to extinction, otters were replaced in Mexican California by cattle hides and tallow bound for the leatherworks of England and the East Coast.

Two missionaries who took a personal and scholarly interest in local tribes left invaluable records of Native cultures and languages. Fray Gerónimo Boscana, of Mission San Juan Capistrano, wrote a lengthy treatise on the Acjachemen (Juaneño) people who lived in the vicinity of his mission. The two surviving versions of this manuscript, titled *Chinigchinich* after a principal deity, furnish extraordinarily detailed descriptions of religious beliefs and social customs

(chapter 11). Fray Felipe Arroyo de la Cuesta, who spent the greater part of his missionary career at Mission San Juan Bautista, compiled grammars and vocabularies for a number of California Indian languages, which have allowed modern descendants to recover voices from their distant past.

Spain's colonization of California nearly destroyed the region's Native cultures, in much the same process suffered worldwide by indigenous peoples who faced expansionist European powers from the fifteenth through the nineteenth centuries. The repercussions of the mission period reverberate today as California Indian descendants work to reclaim their heritage. It seems fitting that colonial documents describing the lives of their mission ancestors are proving to be so important as they strive to reconstruct their history and traditions.

Figure 15.1. The death of Padre Luis Jayme at Mission San Diego during a Native revolt in 1775. Illustration by Alexander Harmer, published in 1920.

Rebellions, Resistance, and Runaways in Colonial Times

Tsim D. Schneider

Evening arrives at Mission San Francisco de Asís, a Franciscan mission more than two thousand miles from Mexico City, at the northernmost reach of New Spain. This calm summer night in 1797 holds no hint of the artificially lighted nights of the future, when automobiles course noisily between burrito joints and bars in the city's Mission District. Yet just as it often does today, thick fog blankets the scene—and tonight it conceals a group of Saclan and Huchiun Indians walking quietly away from the mission grounds. They have had enough of back-breaking labor, short rations, harsh punishments, and rampant disease. For better and for worse, the full moon is at play, illuminating a narrow trail leading down to San Francisco Bay but also casting unwanted shadows as the group slips nervously into the night.

Figure 15.2. Mission San Francisco de Asís as it looks today in downtown San Francisco, California.

Fleeing the missions was only one way in which Native people contended with Spain's effort to bolster its California frontier by taking Indians into the mission complexes, binding them to the Catholic Church through baptism, and turning them into an agrarian workforce loyal to the Crown. Occasionally, mistreatment of Indians at the missions sparked all-out rebellion. Other mission Indians, over time, accepted their new lives (chapter 14). Some picked up skills in working wood, leather, and metal, and some found ways into the families of colonists through caregiving and godparenting.

Excavating former Indian work spaces and dormitories at mission sites, archaeologists find local house styles, chipped stone projectile points, shell beads, and bones from wild animals, together with glass beads, metal tools, and European ceramics. Clearly, new ways did not immediately or completely supplant the old. The mission churches themselves sometimes show the mixing of cultures. At Mission San Francisco, for example, geometric designs painted on the ceiling of the chapel mimic Indian basketry motifs. Many California indigenous communities today still identify with missions as places of ongoing history.

But while some Indians chose to accept mission life, others grew weary of the institutions that once attracted them away from their former villages, ceremonial practices, and subsistence routines. Resistance to Spanish missions took many forms, most of them relatively small acts such as scrawling graffiti on walls, sabotaging mission property, and being tardy for work. Unsurprisingly, these subtler forms of resistance are usually eclipsed in the public's attention by widely circulated accounts of large-scale revolts and violent attacks on missions and missionaries. And such attacks, although relatively rare, did happen.

In 1775, for example, some six hundred Ipai and Tipai from fifteen villages, in a coordinated action, attacked Mission San Diego and bludgeoned the mission's Padre Luis Jayme. Angered by food shortages, harsh punishments, and a string of rapes of Indian women by soldiers, the attackers descended on the mission, looted the church, burned mission buildings, slaughtered cattle, and killed soldiers, a carpenter, and a blacksmith. Then they stripped Padre Jayme naked, shot him full of arrows, and clubbed him to death. Retribution, of course, was swift. Soldiers rounded up Indians from outlying villages, interrogated them, whipped some, and executed others.

Ten years later and a little farther up the coast, an attempted revolt by Gabrielino Tongva people at Mission San Gabriel met only with failure. Sparking the attack, a powerful female shaman named Toypurina prophesied the destruction of Mission San Gabriel and the expulsion of Spaniards from Tongva territory. In a unified assault, Indians from eight villages acted on Toypurina's prophesy and approached the mission at night, bent on eliminating the colonial occupiers. Lying in wait, the mission guard repelled the attack and captured four ringleaders, including Toypurina. At trial she protested the loss of traditional cultural values, abuses by Spaniards, and the occupation of tribal land; another captive complained about prohibitions against dances. These two leaders were banished to opposite ends of California. The other two received prison sentences and were later released.

Violent resistance occasionally erupted in other ways than mass rebellion. Padre Panto, at Mission San Diego, is said to have been poisoned by his cook in 1811 as retribution for being lashed 124 times over a day and a half. Padre Quintana, at Mission Santa Cruz, met a more provocative fate in 1812. Partly in revenge for severe punishments, Indians smothered the padre to death and removed one of his testicles before releasing Native women from their locked dormitory and "frolicking" until the morning hours.

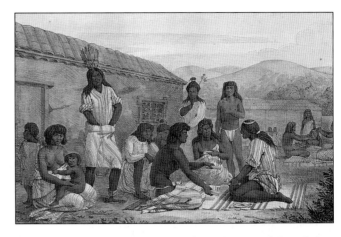

Figure 15.3. *Jeu des habitans de Californie* (Games of the inhabitants of California), watercolor by Louis Choris, 1816. This scene portrays Indians of Mission San Francisco gambling outside their barracks.

Figure 15.4. Interior of the chapel of Mission San Francisco as viewed from the choir loft, showing Native designs painted on the ceiling.

Dramatic flashpoints like these, however, can deflect our attention from subtler but equally significant ways in which Natives responded to colonialism. For thousands of years before Europeans set foot in the Americas, indigenous people had found ways to cope with social, economic, political, and climatic upheavals, sometimes by developing innovative social arrangements and sometimes by moving from one place to another. What we often think of as Native people's "resistance" during colonial times can instead be viewed as a continuation of their long history of successfully negotiating complex social circumstances.

For the most part, Indians of coastal California straddled two worlds during the colonial years.

Figure 15.5. "General Jose Pachito, Captain Pedro Pablo and other captains at a meeting at [Mission San Antonio de] Pala called by the US, July 1885." Native leadership positions at the missions, such as alcaldes and "captains," continued after the missions closed, and such men acted as liaisons between their communities and American colonists.

They relied on material goods of both their own and European manufacture, and they attempted to maintain family connections and traditional trade networks. Even those who violently rebelled at some point might eventually return to the church and the mission way of life. After the failed attack on Mission San Gabriel, for example, the shaman Toypurina was exiled to Monterey, where she later accepted baptism, changed her name, married a *californio* soldier, and bore four children before dying in 1795.

At Mission San Rafael, north of San Francisco, a Coast Miwok man given the name Marino and later called "Chief Marin" served as an indigenous *alcalde*, or appointed magistrate in the mission community. Records show that Marino dutifully attended baptisms in 1823, but padres also labeled him insubordinate. From 1822 to 1824, having left the mission to hide out on an island in San Francisco Bay, he may have spearheaded raids on Spanish properties. Captured from his refuge, Marino ultimately accepted the church by taking the Eucharist at his death in 1832.

A last example is a man named Estanislao, who became alcalde at Mission San José but later fled to the San Joaquin Valley and organized Lakisamni Yokuts people in rebellion against the missions in 1828 and 1829. Estanislao's men repelled a series of punitive expeditions before a final attack led by Lieutenant Mariano G. Vallejo, with an army of californio soldiers and Indian auxiliaries, dislodged the rebels from their marsh hideout. Estanislao returned to Mission San José, where, to Vallejo's anger, the padres granted him asylum. In a complete turnabout, he then took on the job of capturing mission runaways until his death a few years later. The cases of Toypurina, Chief Marin, and Estanislao show that colonial entanglements were complex and that one-time rebels could later accept the Spanish way of life. They also show that mission Indians by no means abandoned all linkages with sympathizers in the hinterland. Mission Indians might still have places of refuge to which they could escape and allies who would help them and even join their cause. The 1824 Chumash revolt is an excellent example, for it speaks to orchestration between Indians residing at missions and those living in outlying, unmissionized communities.

The revolt started after a soldier flogged an Indian from Mission La Purísima who was visiting an imprisoned relative at Mission Santa Inés. Infuriated, Chumash at Mission Santa Inés attacked the garrison with bows and arrows and set buildings ablaze. When more troops arrived the next day, the rebels fled west to Mission La Purísima. Chumash messengers from Santa Inés also carried news of the revolt south to relatives at Mission Santa Barbara, and soon they, too, joined the uprising.

At Santa Barbara, Chumash seized the mission, sacked the priests' quarters, and sent clergy and civilians fleeing to the presidio. Troops then counterattacked and fought a three-hour battle with the insurgents before retreating unexpectedly and allowing the besieged Chumash to slip away into the backcountry. Alcaldes led some of their followers to mountain refuges nearby and eventually farther east to tule marshes in the San Joaquin Valley, where unbaptized Yokuts gave them safe haven. Others, fleeing by canoe, sought refuge on Santa Cruz Island. As so often happened, Franciscan priests eventually persuaded most of the runaways from Santa Barbara to return to the mission.

The Chumash at Mission La Purísima, led in part by alcalde Pacomio Poqui, held out the longest, creating fortifications, arming themselves against californio troops, and even sending sacks of beads to refugees from the other two missions and to chiefs of interior tribes as enticements to continue the revolt. Only after a month-long occupation were they defeated. Colonial authorities executed seven Chumash, sentenced twelve others, including Pacomio, to prison, and killed many more Indians during punitive expeditions. Although handed a sentence of ten years of hard labor, Pacomio seems to have negotiated his term into something more lenient. In a pattern familiar by now, he took up residence with his family in Monterey and—perhaps with a changed outlook on the church—became a skilled carpenter and furniture maker.

Figure 15.6. *Californio* soldiers battling Chumash Indians at Mission Santa Barbara during the Chumash revolt of 1824. Illustration by Alexander Harmer, published in 1923.

Outright rebellion, for all its drama, was in fact the less common way for Indians to challenge the missions. More often, they fled without permission, like the mixed group of Saclan and Huchiun speakers whom I depicted at the beginning of this chapter. Leaving Mission San Francisco in 1797 as part of a single exodus of 280 baptized Indians, they headed for home villages and other places of refuge in and around present-day Oakland and Berkeley. In other years, Indians fleeing San Francisco Bay missions traveled even farther east, to the vast tule marshes of the Sacramento and San Joaquin Valleys and beyond. One researcher estimated that between 5 and 10 percent of the seventy thousand Indians baptized at the California missions fled over the course of the mission period. Although the number probably varied from year to year, depending on the leniency of the padres and other factors, the rate of departure confirms that mission Indians did not completely abandon their indigenous communities but maintained useful linkages with them.

Escapees' reasons for leaving were legion. Some

of the Saclan and Huchiun Indians who fled Mission San Francisco in 1797 were captured, brought back to San Francisco, and interrogated about why they had left. Their recorded interviews speak to hard labor, extreme punishments, temperamental padres and Native overseers, food shortages, and other difficulties of life at the missions. The close quarters of mission barracks—in the case of San Francisco, exacerbated by the cool, damp climate—were breeding grounds for tuberculosis and venereal diseases. Consistently high death rates, dysentery caused by drinking contaminated water, and poor living conditions drove mission Indians to try to return to their old ways of life in the hinterlands. Mission administrators continually had to recruit new or returning Indians to the missions in order to keep them operational, even while instating measures to prevent open hostility and revolt.

Just as the Indians had to adapt to survive in Spanish and Mexican California, so did the missionaries. In arid southern California, where it was hard to grow enough crops to feed an entire mission community, the padres allowed some Indians to remain in their home villages and travel to the missions just for masses, feasts, and other events. Replies to a questionnaire circulated among the California missions between 1813 and 1815 show that Indians still had opportunities to continue some traditional

Figure 15.7. Mission La Purísima (La Purísima Mission State Historic Park), scene of intense fighting during the 1824 Chumash revolt.

routines. Padres at Mission Santa Barbara, for example, remarked that when hollyleaf cherries ripened in the fall, Indians associated with the missions lived scattered in the surrounding hills, picking fruit.

Eventually, some missions instituted a furlough system called *paseo*, or "promenade," under which Indians could return to their home villages and supplement their mission rations with locally available food. This unstandardized form of approved leave helped circumvent a few of the big pitfalls of mission life, such as food shortages and homesickness. The padres also hoped the returnees would advertise the mission lifestyle to ambivalent relatives. Native people had their unspoken agendas, too. New documentary research has revealed that Indians at Mission San Francisco strategically timed their paseos to coincide with birth and death rites forbidden by the Catholic Church.

Researchers today, besides reassessing the opportunities Indians had to leave the missions, are looking beyond the mission walls to better understand the places to which Indians traveled when they left. For instance, in the hills of Kern County, east of Santa Barbara and far from the coastal missions, archaeologists are investigating the camps of Indian runaways, some of them situated within a few feet of centuries-old rock art. Near the rock art panels, excavators have found deposits of mixed marine shell beads and glass beads, suggesting that the runaways were reinvesting themselves in ancestral places even while partaking of novel materials.

My own excavations at three shell mounds north of Mission San Francisco, in present-day Marin County, show that Indians may have used some mounds not solely in pre-Columbian times but also as late as the mission period, judging from new radiocarbon dates (chapter 6). Yet the glass beads, European pottery, and other imported items that archaeologists find at most mission-period sites are absent from these three mounds. Their absence inspires further thinking about the things Indians brought with them or left behind when visiting places of refuge in the hinterland. Perhaps like those who departed for the Marin shell mounds, the Saclan and Huchiun Indians who fled to the East Bay in 1797 purposefully left their European goods behind.

From San Diego to San Francisco Bay, Native people engaged with Spanish missions in ways far more complicated than either solely succumbing to or resisting an imposed way of life. Researchers are now exploring a veritable spectrum of decisions Indians made in accepting, refusing, or modifying the material goods and modes of living introduced by Spanish colonialism. More than revolt and the murder of missionaries, resistance to the missions entailed myriad historically and culturally rooted decisions made as situations continually changed. The padres, too, had to adapt to California's peoples and environments, sometimes by implementing measures such as approved furloughs that deviated from colonial mandate. Even the individual personalities of the padres influenced decisions about whether Indians might temporarily leave the missions or reside in their home villages.

Understanding something of the fluidity of people's coming and going around the missions has led scholars also to think more about the landscapes encircling them. New research on indigenous hinterlands suggests they were places where Native people retained and renewed their culture, reengaged with traditional villages and sacred sites, and—away from the padres' watchful eyes—developed ways to overcome the challenges of their time.

Figure 16.1. Two redwood boxes and a whale rib marker the authors found eroding from a sea cliff on San Nicolas Island. One end of the larger box at right had been lost to erosion.

Rising Seas, Coastal Erosion, and Archaeological Discovery

Jon M. Erlandson and René L. Vellanoweth

Along California's golden shores, the sea takes a steady toll. Scenic cliffs, seemingly as stable as the stone they are made of, slowly retreat from the relentless onslaught of surf, storms, gravity, and human modification of the shoreline. As the world warms, global sea levels are rising relatively rapidly. The advancing sea endangers thousands of archaeological sites, and with them a record of fifteen thousand years of human history. The loss of our communal maritime history is turning potentially catastrophic.

For many of the past thirty years we have been racing this rising tide, working with federal and state agencies, coastal tribes, and other partners to monitor coastal erosion, date threatened sites, and perform a kind of historical triage by salvaging data from the most threatened and important sites. We have explored twelve-thousand-year-old Paleocoastal sites (chapter 2), nineteenth-century ranching sites and Chinese abalone middens, mid-twentieth-century military sites, and virtually everything in between.

In 2009 our efforts paid amazing dividends on San Nicolas Island, where Nicoleño, or Island Tongva, people lived for millennia before being removed to the mainland by order of Franciscan padres in 1835. Hints of an even deeper human history on San Nicolas came from our discovery of chipped stone crescents, distinctive artifacts that date between approximately twelve thousand and eight thousand years ago on the Northern Channel Islands. Searching for such evidence of Paleocoastal people, we were following deeply buried soils eroding from beneath sand dunes deposited after about six thousand years ago. Exposed in sea cliffs and canyon walls, these soils were older than the many large shell middens that cap the dunes and mark the village and campsites of the Nicoleños.

Walking along a sheer sea cliff, one of us looked down and spotted a whale rib eroding from a fossil beach deposit. Thinking the rib was a fossil, we were surprised to find that the large bone had been placed intentionally over two old redwood boxes, part of a cultural feature eroding rapidly from the cliff face. One end of the larger box had fallen off, exposing artifacts including a large abalone shell, a soapstone tube bead, a brass button, and an old piece of green bottle glass. Nearby lay a fragment of a woven basketry water bottle coated with tar (asphaltum) to make it watertight.

After consulting with our colleagues Lisa Barnett-Thomas (US Navy) and Troy Davis (University of Oregon), we halted our coastal survey and gathered the equipment we would need to salvage the boxes before they were lost to winter storms. The next morning in the field, we saw hints of the incredible array of artifacts the boxes contained: numerous local Nicoleño objects made from shell, bone, stone, and wood; a handful of metal and glass objects of European or Euroamerican origin; and several bone harpoon points of Native Alaskan origin.

Behind the boxes we found two whole, asphaltum-coated water bottles, one large and one small.

A full accounting of the richness of our discovery would await the meticulous excavation of the boxes' contents in the laboratory that winter, when Vellanoweth, Thomas-Barnett, and US Navy archaeologist Steven Schwartz identified and cataloged more than two

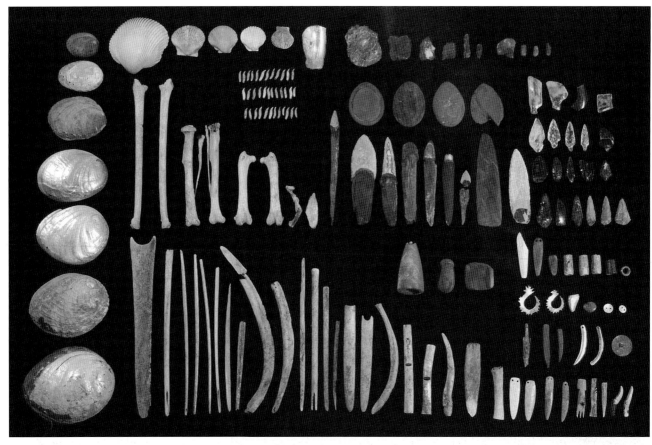

Figure 16.2. The contents of the larger redwood box, including abalone shell dishes and other marine shells, modified and unmodified animal bones and teeth, hafted stone knives, stone and glass projectile points, two stylized abalone shell fishhooks, a variety of ornaments and effigies, and a red stone pipe.

hundred artifacts of stone, bone, shell, metal, and glass. These included extraordinary finds rarely seen by archaeologists, professional or amateur: hafted knives with redwood handles and stone blades; projectile points chipped from glass; a pipe carved from red stone with a wad of unburned tobacco in its bowl; a variety of bone pins and ornaments; two uniquely barbed fishhooks made from abalone shell; and much more.

How did this remarkable collection of artifacts come to be hidden in a sea cliff alcove? We have not yet completed our analyses of the cache, but we currently believe that a Nicoleño person used the boxes during the early to mid-1800s. At the time, the California coast, like much of the rest of the world, was being changed dramatically by European colonialism and globalization, leading to a clash of cultures that is reflected in the contents of these unique boxes. The presence of Koniag-style toggling harpoons

and other artifacts from the Pacific Northwest tells us that the boxes were used after Russian-led parties of Native Alaskan sea otter hunters visited San Nicolas Island in 1814 and 1815, reportedly killing many of the Nicoleño men. The boxes themselves were made in Nicoleño fashion from redwood planks glued together with asphaltum, without nails, screws, or metal wire. Clearly, they were used before 1853, when the last Nicoleño person—the famed Juana Maria, also known as the "Lone Woman of San Nicolas"—was removed to the mainland after living alone on the island for eighteen years.

Although we cannot be certain, it is entirely possible that the sea cliff hideaway was stocked by Juana Maria herself, whose fictionalized life story was memorialized by Scott O'Dell in his award-winning 1966 book *Island of the Blue Dolphins* and later in a Hollywood movie of the same name. Whether the boxes were left by Juana Maria or her

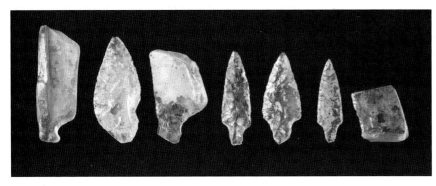

Figure 16.3. Clear glass artifacts from the redwood boxes. The artifact at left is approximately two and a half inches long.

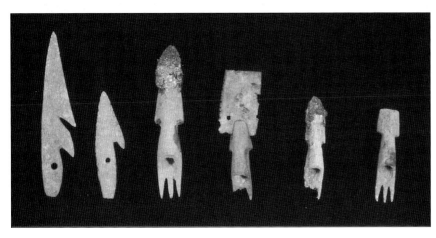

Figure 16.4. Six Native Alaskan–style harpoon points, including three toggling harpoons in the center with intact metal blades. The point at left is approximately four inches long.

Nicoleño tribal members, their amazing contents provide a rare opportunity to explore the connections between archaeology, history, and the lives of real people caught up in the tumult of California's early historic years.

Racing a rising tide, responding with a systematic shoreline survey, we were fortunate to find such a remarkable time capsule, which tells us much about the complex history of the California coast. All around the world, rising seas and accelerating erosion are destroying archaeological sites that similarly contain priceless records of our ancestors' deep maritime history. Along the California coast and beyond, more resources, partnerships, and efforts are needed to preserve, protect, and salvage those endangered archaeological sites.

Acknowledgments

Our work on San Nicolas Island was supported by the United States Navy; California State University, Los Angeles; and the University of Oregon. We are indebted to Steve Schwartz, Lisa Barnett-Thomas, and numerous students and colleagues who have helped preserve and analyze the contents of the San Nicolas Island cache feature. We are also grateful for the support and encouragement we have received from many Tongva tribal members.

Figure 17.1. Linda Yamane collecting willows for basketry. "I look happy," she says, "because after many years of searching, I had finally found an abundant source of beautiful sandbar willow."

Weaving the Past into the Present

seventeen

Linda Yamane

In rolling coastal woodlands and dry stream beds, along lush riverbanks and roadsides, in little-noticed places, the roots, shoots, and stems of certain native plants are lovingly harvested by a small but dedicated army of California Indian basket weavers. Like our ancestors before us, we gather ordinary plants from nature and transform them into beautiful baskets, an art reaching back thousands of years in time.

In the past, baskets were an essential part of everyday life. They cradled babies, held one's belongings, and carried heavy loads. People needed them to harvest, prepare, serve, and store foods and to transport and store water. Often they accompanied a person to his or her grave. They filled the same needs that today's pots and pans, cups and bowls, bags and backpacks, storage containers and baby carriers now fill. Feathered ceremonial baskets appeared in religious ceremonies and on special occasions such as the honoring of important guests. Today, weaving baskets is a way of bringing honor and respect to our ancestors and of keeping our culture alive.

My Rumsien Ohlone ancestors lived in villages in what is now Monterey and Carmel Valley, California, for several thousand years before Spaniards and other Europeans came to settle the California coast. Franciscan missions and Spanish ranchos brought traumatic and irreversible changes to tribal life. In order to survive these horrific times, families had to leave behind many traditions, including basket making.

That's why I didn't grow up with the baskets of my Ohlone ancestors. A small number of Ohlone elders,

Figure 17.2. Created from the natural gifts of the land, such as this coastal woodland, California Indian baskets are among the ancestors' greatest aesthetic achievements.

born at Mission San Carlos, knew how to weave our people's utilitarian baskets, but when they died in the 1800s, that knowledge slipped away from this world with them.

By the time I was born, most of those women had been gone for nearly a hundred years. I believe they had continued to make utilitarian twined baskets because that type remained useful for preparing food in mission times and afterward. But I know of no one who wove the kind of intricate coiled baskets our ancestors made, which had no practical value in the new regime—especially the fancy feathered ones. The enormous number of labor hours required to make them would have kept a woman away from her mission "duties" for much too long.

Yet some of these spectacular baskets still existed in mission and post-mission times, and a few visitors made special note of them in their travel journals. After visiting Monterey for nearly a month in October 1837, the Frenchman Abel du Petit-Thouars wrote, "These natives…make baskets in the form of plates and graceful cups which they ornament on the outside with black feathers from the top-knots of the California partridge, with other feathers of different colors, and with little pearly shells."

A few feathered Ohlone and Coast Miwok baskets, acquired by visitors as souvenirs from central California, made their way to Europe and later became part of national museum collections. A handful of such baskets reside in American museums on the East Coast, and one recently came home to California. But altogether, probably fewer than forty Ohlone baskets of all types remain in the world. With no living basket weavers to learn from, I turned to the baskets themselves as my teachers when I wanted to start making baskets, and sometimes I had to travel great distances to visit them.

I never thought I would be able to make a traditional Ohlone basket, having read that all our baskets had "perished." Later, when I learned that a few had in fact survived, I set out to track them down in museum collections. I began by visiting the few baskets in California, photographing them closely and taking technical notes.

I learned from other California weavers how to gather and prepare the native plants used in baskets, and then I spent several years scouting for those plants

Figure 17.3. The author's first traditional basket, dedicated to her grandmother Beatrice Barcelon, a gifted storyteller. Both Barcelon and her mother, Alta Gracia Soto, were artists and herbalists who influenced Yamane's creative nature and connected her to her Native roots.

in the Monterey area, where I live. Fortunately, I had been a fiber artist in my twenties, so my hands already knew the basketry techniques of coiling and twining. Quickly, I learned to work with traditional plant materials. In 1994, at the age of forty-five, I completed my first small basket—the first Ohlone basket to be made in about 150 years. Because of my deep love for and connection to my grandmother, I desperately wanted to give my first basket to her. I knew that as a woman who also made things with her hands, she would have been proud. But she had already passed on, so I gave it to her the best way I could, by placing her picture inside the basket, where it has lived ever since.

I continued weaving, expanding my experience and taking on new challenges. Next I made a *walaheen*, a twined seed-roasting basket unique to the southern Ohlone area. After photographing one in a San Jose museum collection, I enlarged the photographs so I could count sticks and stitches and analyze the pattern. A year and a half later it was finished, the first Ohlone seed roaster to be made in more than a century.

When people think about what it takes to make a basket, they usually think only of the weaving itself. But an enormous amount of work must be done before weaving can ever begin. First, the proper plants must

Figure 17.4. Yamane gathering olive shells for beads. Working at low tide, she is ever mindful of the capricious waves and rising tide that can easily trap her in her favorite cove.

then the bark adheres, so I simply dry the sticks with the bark intact. Before my willows are ready for coiled weaving, I must scrape each one to a uniform diameter with a sharp knife.

The other plant most important to Ohlone basketry is a sedge whose scientific name is *Carex barbarae*. I work on hands and knees among its slender leaves, digging the earth in search of its long rhizomes, which travel beneath the surface and connect one plant to another. I then excavate the sturdy runners to their full length before clipping them free, leaving the plants to continue their growth. It takes many, many hours of physical labor to harvest enough material for a single basket.

be gathered, and in today's world they are not always easy to find. Limited access to necessary materials has long been a threat to the continuity of California Indian basketry. It has taken me years to resolve the problem of finding the plants I need, and sometimes I have difficulty doing so even today.

Ohlone baskets are made primarily of willow shoots and sedge rhizomes. Bulrush and bracken fern runners form the dark patterns in some baskets. The willow shoots used in California Indian basketry must be straight and smooth, without any lateral branches or insect damage. The species used in Ohlone baskets are arroyo willow and sandbar, or narrowleaf, willow, both members of the genus *Salix*, with a narrow inner pith. For the fine work of coiled baskets, sandbar willow is a must. When I harvest it in the spring, I remove the bark and tie the sticks into bundles to keep them straight as they dry for several months. If I gather it in the winter, when the sap has dropped,

When my work is done, I close the ground, replacing the leaves and other plant debris that blanketed the surface. If gathering in the heat of summer, I sprinkle water on the area I've disturbed, in order to replace precious moisture lost when I opened the ground. For California Indian basket weavers, it's important to show respect for the plants and for the earth by saying thank you. In my Rumsien language, I sing a song of thanks. Sometimes I leave other gifts, such as glittering bits of abalone shell.

While the sedge runners are still fresh and moist, I split each one in half lengthwise to expose the light-colored, woody strand within. It takes practice, patience, and a delicate touch to split these properly. Then I remove the bark and bundle the strands so they can dry for several months. Later, I soak them in water, then scrape and trim each one. Only after careful manicuring are they ready for the weaving itself.

Over the years I produced a number of different kinds of baskets, but in 2009 I undertook my most demanding project yet—that of making two ceremonial baskets, the most difficult of all Ohlone basketry. The Oakland Museum of California commissioned one of the pieces, and a grant from the Creative Work Fund supported the other. Meticulously, I decorated these ceremonial baskets with patternwork of tiny shell disk beads and red feathers, which I incorporated into the stitches of the basket as I wove (plates 6 and 7). In addition to the normal routines of gathering and preparing plant materials and then the weaving

Figure 17.5. An old Ohlone basket, one of the few examples of its kind remaining in the United States, which the author studied at the Smithsonian Institution. It once belonged to a family from Santa Clara, California, and is still magnificent despite the loss of most of its decorative featherwork to insect damage.

itself, these special baskets required me to make more than two thousand sequinlike shell beads with which to form the exterior patterns. I had seen such beads in museum exhibits and archaeological reports and had handled a few during reburials and in archaeological situations. But it was another thing altogether to be faced with gathering enough raw material and producing so many of them myself. I also met with technical challenges when it came time to weave them into the stitches of the basket.

I make such beads from the shells of a small sea snail that biologists call *Olivella biplicata*, which I search for at low tide, choosing only the white-colored ones. I am careful to take only empty shells, not live snails. I first heat the shells in hot sand, which whitens them further and makes them less brittle. Next, I break each shell with a hammer stone, saving pieces of the right size and contour. I then clip each piece into a roughly circular shape, after which it's time to drill the hole. Finally, I grind the bead smooth and round with an electric grinding tool. It takes about fifteen minutes per bead, and the two baskets I began in 2009 required about twenty-two hundred beads. In the hope of speeding up the process, I experimented by stringing short stacks of beads onto a length of wire, which I ground by rolling it on a slab of sandstone.

But the concave shape of the olive shell resulted in a rough edge, which I didn't like, so I continued to grind each bead individually.

The feathers posed their own problems. In ancient times, my Ohlone ancestors used red feathers from the scalp of the acorn woodpecker. But because of legal issues and the obvious difficulty of obtaining enough woodpecker feathers—even if I could have arranged for a special permit—I decided to substitute chicken feathers, which I dyed and then clipped and snipped to an appropriate size.

Before I could begin making the two new ceremonial baskets, I needed to visit some older ones, to study and learn from them. I traveled to the Smithsonian Institution in Washington, DC, the American Museum of Natural History in New York City, the British Museum in London, and the Musée du Quai Branly in Paris. During these visits, I measured olive shell beads, counted and measured stitches, studied starts and finishes, and paid special attention to feathers. I took lots of photos for later study. It was intense work but incredibly exciting to meet these baskets, which had left California some two hundred years earlier. In private moments I talked to them softly in the Rumsien language, hoping it would stir their memories of home.

Figure 17.6. The author at work on one of her two ceremonial baskets, incorporating beads and feathers into the stitches, one by one.

Most of the feathers on the old baskets are missing, having been eaten away by moths over the centuries, and those that remain are sometimes faded. But the baskets are beautiful nonetheless, and I tried to visualize how they must have looked in their full, feathered glory. I imagined the hands of the basket weavers of our villages, strong and confident, following tradition yet leaving their own unique and creative touches on each basket.

It took three arduous years, but day by day, bead by bead, feather by feather, and stitch by stitch, I eventually completed the two ceremonial baskets, the first to be made in about 250 years. I finally found myself weaving the last row in the wee hours of the morning. As I reached the end and was wrapping the last stitches around the tapered willow rods, I saw something I hadn't seen before. I saw the basket in its completeness, and in that instant I realized something I knew was a truth. The basket is a prayer. Not a prayer with words. The basket, itself, is a prayer.

The making of these baskets was truly a journey—from my first days twenty-odd years before, when I learned to find, prepare, and weave with traditional materials, to my visits to museums on the East Coast and in Europe. During those years I faced many challenges and endured endless hours of tedious repetition. But the rarity of Ohlone basketry makes its revival important and poignant for our people today. Baskets are helping to reunite a cultural community that was disrupted and displaced by the circumstances of history. Baskets are also emerging as an invaluable teaching tool, informing us about the past while deepening our bonds with each other and with the land.

I am not alone in my efforts. California Indian basket weavers from many tribes are working to keep their ancient traditions alive in the twenty-first century. Some communities have been fortunate to sustain an unbroken chain of basket weavers across the generations, and young people can learn their weaving traditions directly from them. Other weavers have dedicated years to finding and studying the baskets of their people, learning the plants and the weaving techniques and breathing new life into an ancient art form that once flourished in every community in California.

I gather my basket sticks and roots along the Carmel River near my ancestral village, knowing that my great-grandmothers and great-aunties gathered their basket materials in the same places before me. When I make the little olive shell beads, I know that my great-grandfathers and great-uncles made them with their hands before me. They walked on the same earth and the same ocean beaches, and I am honored to follow in their footsteps, keeping their traditions and their memory alive.

Suggested Reading

Anderson, M. Kat
2005   *Tending the Wild: Native American Knowledge and the Management of California's Natural Resources.* University of California Press, Berkeley.

Bibby, Brian
2012   *Essential Art: Native Basketry from the California Indian Heritage Center.* Heyday, Berkeley.

Blackburn, Thomas C.
1975   *December's Child: A Book of Chumash Oral Narratives.* University of California Press, Berkeley.

Blackburn, Thomas C., and M. Kat Anderson, editors
1993   *Before the Wilderness: Environmental Management by Native Californians.* Ballena Press, Menlo Park, California.

Boscana, Gerónimo
2005   *Chinigchinich: A Revised and Annotated Version of Alfred Robinson's Translation of Father Gerónimo Boscana's Historical Account of the Belief, Usages, Customs, and Extravagancies of the Indians of This Mission of San Juan Capistrano Called the Acagchemem Tribe.* Annotations by John P. Harrington; reprinted with William Bright's 1978 preface and 2005 introduction by John Johnson. Malki Museum Press, Banning, California.

Brown, Alan K.
2001   *A Description of Distant Roads: Original Journals of the First Expedition into California 1769–1770 by Juan Crespí.* San Diego State University Press.

Erlandson, Jon M., Torben C. Rick, Terry L. Jones, and Judith F. Porcasi
2007   "One if by Land, Two if by Sea: Who Were the First Californians?" In *California Prehistory: Colonization, Culture, and Complexity,* edited by Terry L. Jones and Kathryn A. Klar, pp. 53–62. Altamira Press, Lanham, Maryland.

Fagan, Brian
2013   *The Attacking Ocean: The Past, Present, and Future of Rising Sea Levels.* Bloomsbury Press, New York.

Gamble, Lynn H.
2008   *The Chumash World at European Contact: Power, Trade, and Feasting among Complex Hunter-Gatherers.* University of California Press, Berkeley.

Golla, Victor
2011   *California Indian Languages.* University of California Press, Berkeley.

Grant, Campbell
1965   *The Rock Paintings of the Chumash: A Study of a California Indian Culture.* University of California Press, Berkeley.

Hackel, Steven W.
2005   *Children of Coyote, Missionaries of Saint Francis: Indian-Spanish Relations in Colonial California, 1769–1850.* Published for the Omohundro Institute of Early American History and Culture, Williamsburg, Virginia. University of North Carolina Press, Chapel Hill.

Hudson, Travis, Janice Timbrook, and Melissa Rempe
1978   *Tomol: Chumash Watercraft as Described in the Ethnographic Notes of John P. Harrington.* Ballena Press, Socorro, New Mexico.

Hudson, Travis, and Ernest Underhay
1978   *Crystals in the Sky: An Intellectual Odyssey Involving Chumash Astronomy, Cosmology, and Rock Art.* Ballena Press, Socorro, New Mexico.

Jackson, Robert H., and Edward Castillo
1995   *Indians, Franciscans, and Spanish Colonization: The Impact of the Mission System on California Indians.* University of New Mexico Press, Albuquerque.

Jones, Terry L., Nathan E. Stevens, Deborah A. Jones, Richard T. Fitzgerald, and Mark G. Hylkema
2007   "The Central Coast: A Mid-latitude Milieu." In *California Prehistory: Colonization, Culture, and Complexity,* edited by Terry L. Jones and Kathryn A. Klar, pp. 125–146. Altamira Press, Lanham, Maryland.

Kimbro, Edna E., and Julia G. Costello
2009   *The California Missions: History, Art, and Preservation.* Getty Conservation Institute, Los Angeles.

Lightfoot, Kent G.
2005   *Indians, Missionaries, and Merchants: The Legacy of Colonial Encounters on the California Frontiers.* University of California Press, Berkeley.

Lightfoot, Kent G., and Otis Parrish
2009   *California Indians and Their Environment: An Introduction.* University of California Press, Berkeley.

Masters, Patricia M., and Ivano W. Aiello
2007   "Postglacial Evolution of Coastal Environments." In *California Prehistory: Colonization, Culture, and Complexity,* edited by Terry L. Jones and Kathryn A. Klar, pp. 35–51. Altamira Press, Lanham, Maryland.

McCawley, William
1996   *The First Angelinos: The Gabrielino Indians of Los Angeles.* Malki Museum Press/Ballena Press Cooperative Publication, Banning, California.

Webb, Edith Buckland
2004   *Indian Life at the Old Missions.* Blackburn Press, Caldwell, New Jersey.

About the Authors

Jeffrey H. Altschul is a member of Statistical Research, Inc. (SRI), and its Playa Vista Archaeological and Historical Project. In 1989 he began SRI's research program in the Ballona wetland, which to date has led to the excavation of more than a dozen archaeological sites.

Richard Ciolek-Torello is a member of Statistical Research, Inc. (SRI), and its Playa Vista Archaeological and Historical Project. He helped design SRI's research program in the Ballona and oversaw many of its excavations.

Julia G. Costello is an archaeologist who has worked for more than three decades on sites related to the Spanish and Mexican occupations of California and their effects on Native populations. Her studies of sites of missions, ranchos, presidios, and pueblos have provided new insights into California's colonial history.

Rob Q. Cuthrell is a postdoctoral fellow at the University of California, Berkeley, studying indigenous landscape management practices in California through archaeobotany and paleoecology.

Matthew Des Lauriers is an associate professor of anthropology at California State University, Northridge. He has conducted research in Baja California since 2000, primarily on Isla Cedros, situated off the Pacific coast of the peninsula.

John G. Douglass is a member of Statistical Research, Inc. (SRI), and its Playa Vista Archaeological and Historical Project. He is also a visiting scholar in the School of Anthropology at the University of Arizona. He has directed archaeological investigations at a number of sites in the Ballona area, including the Del Rey site.

Jon M. Erlandson is an archaeologist, a professor of anthropology, and director of the Museum of Natural and Cultural History at the University of Oregon. He was born and raised on the California coast, where he has worked for more than thirty-five years with government agencies and tribal members to help preserve archaeological sites.

Lynn H. Gamble is an archaeologist and professor of anthropology at the University of California, Santa Barbara. She studies the emergence of sociopolitical complexity among hunting-and-gathering peoples of California by examining their exchange systems, religious organization, hierarchy, and cultural landscapes. Her book *The Chumash World at European Contact* draws on archaeology, historical documents, ethnography, and ecology to reconstruct daily life among the Chumash Indians of the Santa Barbara Channel.

Michael A. Glassow is a professor emeritus in the Department of Anthropology at the University of California, Santa Barbara. A specialist in California archaeology, he has focused his research on the ecological adaptations of the pre-Columbian people who lived in the Santa Barbara Channel region.

Donn R. Grenda is a member of Statistical Research, Inc. (SRI), and its Playa Vista Archaeological and Historical Project. He led the excavation of the Ballona archaeological site LAN-62, among others.

William Hyder is a research associate of the Santa Barbara Museum of Natural History, having retired from administrative work at the University of California, Santa Cruz, in 2010. He has served as president of the American Rock Art Research Association, has edited, written, and co-authored numerous rock art publications, and has conducted independent rock art studies for the National Park Service, the California State Parks, and private corporations.

Mark G. Hylkema is the Santa Cruz District archaeologist with California State Parks and an adjunct professor of anthropology at Foothill College in Los Altos Hills.

John R. Johnson is an archaeologist who has served as curator of anthropology at the Santa Barbara Museum of Natural History since 1986 and holds an appointment as adjunct professor of anthropology at the University of California, Santa Barbara. He uses primary records from the mission period to reconstruct the settlement patterns, sociopolitical organization, and demographic history of California Indians.

Terry L. Jones is a professor of anthropology and chair of the Department of Social Sciences at California Polytechnic State University, San Luis Obispo, where he has taught for the last sixteen years. He has been involved in archaeological field research on the central California coast for the last thirty years.

Georgia Lee is a research associate of the Santa Barbara Museum of Natural History and the author of many books and articles about rock art. In California she has studied Chumash Indian rock art sites as well as sites in adjacent tribal areas, including Lava Beds National Monument. Earlier she conducted extensive fieldwork on Easter Island and made a definitive study of rock carvings and paintings in the Hawaiian Islands.

Kent G. Lightfoot is a professor of anthropology at the University of California, Berkeley. He has worked on archaeological projects in the American Southwest, New England, and California.

Edward M. Luby is director of the Museum Studies Program and a professor of museum studies at San Francisco State University. Before holding this position, he worked for ten years at the University of California, Berkeley, where he most recently served as associate director of the Berkeley Natural History Museums.

Patricia Masters has published more than fifty scientific papers in biogeochemistry, environmental organic chemistry, marine archaeology, and reconstructions of coastal paleo-environments. She co-edited the book *Quaternary Coastlines and Marine Archaeology* and developed the website www.coastalchange.ucsd.edu.

Jennifer E. Perry is an anthropology professor at California State University, Channel Islands. She is interested in interactions between humans and their environment over time, especially in coastal settings, and her current research is focused on the Channel Islands. Her most recent publication is the edited volume *California's Channel Islands: The Archaeology of Human-Environment Interactions*.

Judith F. Porcasi, after working for nearly thirty years in the southern California aerospace engineering industry, found a rewarding second career in archaeology, concentrating her skills in zooarchaeology on the marine mammals of the California coast. She currently works in the Zooarchaeology Lab of the Cotsen Institute of Archaeology at the University of California, Los Angeles, and also serves as a private consultant to cultural resource management firms.

Seetha N. Reddy is the owner of Reddy Anthropological Consulting. Previously a member of Statistical Research, Inc. (SRI), and its Playa Vista Archaeological and Historical Project, she helped lead the analysis and reporting of many key sites in the Ballona wetland and analyzed hundreds of thousands of seeds as part of that research.

Torben C. Rick is a curator and research scientist in the Department of Anthropology at the Smithsonian Institution's National Museum of Natural History. Working in coastal California, the Chesapeake Bay, and the Pacific Northwest, he has studied coastal and island archaeology and historical ecology. Most of his current research deals with understanding past and present interactions between humans and the environment.

Matthew A. Russell works in cultural resources management in the San Francisco Bay area. From 1993 to 2011 he worked as an archaeologist with the National Park Service's Submerged Resources Center.

Tsim D. Schneider is an assistant professor of anthropology at the University of California, Santa Cruz, and a citizen of the Federated Indians of Graton Rancheria. His continuing archaeological research investigates Native refuge from Spanish missions and other responses to colonialism in the San Francisco Bay area of California.

Chuck J. Striplen is an associate environmental scientist at the San Francisco Estuary Institute (SFEI) and a member of the Amah Mutsun Tribal Band. At SFEI, he most recently developed a cultural landscapes program, designed in part to facilitate better collaborative research between tribes and the scientific community around watershed and cultural resource protection.

Heather B. Thakar is an assistant professor of anthropology and director of the Anthropology Laboratory at Temple University. Her research interests encompass pre-Columbian coastal hunter-gatherers throughout California and Mexico and the ways in which they interacted with, understood, and related to their environment.

René L. Vellanoweth, an archaeologist, is a professor and chair of the Department of Anthropology at California State University, Los Angeles. He has worked on California's Channel Islands for more than twenty years.

Linda Yamane is a California Indian basket weaver, singer, artist, author, and storyteller who traces her ancestry to the Rumsien Ohlone, the Native people of Carmel Valley. She has spent twenty-five years researching Ohlone history and reviving Rumsien language, song, folklore, basketry, and other traditions that were once thought lost.

Picture Credits

Color section, after page 36: Plate 1, courtesy Santa Barbara Museum of Natural History; photo by Bill Zeldis. Plates 2, 4, 8, 12, 22, 23, and 24, courtesy Macduff Everton, photographer. Plate 3, courtesy Santa Barbara Historical Museum. Plate 5, courtesy Phoebe A. Hearst Museum of Anthropology and Regents of the University of California, catalog no. 1-30477; photo by Lynn H. Gamble. Plates 6 and 7, courtesy Linda Yamane, photographer. Plates 9 and 18, courtesy Rick Bury, photographer. Plate 10, courtesy Gordon Miller, artist. Plate 11, courtesy Robert V. Schwemmer, photographer, Channel Islands National Marine Sanctuary, National Oceanic and Atmospheric Administration. Plate 13, © 1977 Mort Künstler, Inc., *Kuksu Ceremony of the Pomo*, courtesy Mort Künstler, artist. Plate 14, courtesy Statistical Research, Inc. Plate 15, courtesy Russell Clay Ruiz. Plate 16, courtesy Lynn H. Gamble, photographer. Plate 17, courtesy David W. Rickman, artist. Plates 19 and 21, courtesy William D. Hyder, photographer. Plate 20, courtesy Phelan Collection at the Santa Barbara Museum of Natural History; photo by Lynn H. Gamble.

Front matter: Map by Molly O'Halloran.

Chapter One: Fig. 1.1, Edward S. Curtis Collection, Library of Congress, Washington, D.C., neg. no. LC-USZ62-116525. Fig. 1.2, published in Georg H. von Langsdorff, *Voyages and Travels in Various Parts of the World, During the Years 1803, 1804, 1805, 1806, and 1807*, vol. 2. (London: Henry Colburn, 1814); courtesy Bancroft Library, University of California, Berkeley. Figs. 1.3 and 1.4, courtesy John Carter Library, Brown University. Fig. 1.5, courtesy Glenn Russell, photographer. Fig. 1.6, courtesy Lynn H. Gamble, photographer.

Chapter Two: Fig. 2.1, courtesy Antonio Busiello, photographer. Fig. 2.2, courtesy Douglas Kennett. Fig. 2.3, courtesy Santa Barbara Museum of Natural History. Figs. 2.4 and 2.7, courtesy Jon Erlandson, photographer. Figs. 2.5 and 2.6, composite digital scans by K. Hamm and J. Erlandson.

Chapter Three: Fig. 3.1, courtesy Gary E. Davis, photographer, www.GEDApix.com. Fig. 3.2, courtesy Adam Young, Scripps Institution of Oceanography. Fig. 3.3, courtesy Douglas L. Inman, Scripps Institution of Oceanography. Fig. 3.4, © Phillip Colla / Oceanlight.com, all rights reserved worldwide. Figs. 3.5 and 3.6, courtesy P. M. Masters, photographer.

Chapter Four: Figs. 4.1 and 4.2, courtesy Rick Flores, University of California, Santa Cruz Arboretum. Fig. 4.3, courtesy Rob Cuthrell and ESRI. Figs. 4.4 and 4.5, courtesy Chuck Striplen. Figs. 4.6 and 4.7, courtesy Rob Cuthrell.

Chapter Five: Figs. 5.1 and 5.4, courtesy Frank Magallanes and Althea Edwards, photographers. Fig. 5.2, courtesy Bancroft Library, University of California, Berkeley. Fig. 5.3, courtesy Lutisuc Asociación Cultural IAP; photo by Alberto Mellado Moreno, Punta Chueca Seri community. Fig. 5.5, courtesy Santa Barbara Museum of Natural History.

Chapter Six: Fig. 6.1, courtesy American Museum of Natural History Library, New York. Figs. 6.2 and 6.3, courtesy Phoebe A. Hearst Museum of Anthropology and Regents of the University of California, catalog nos. 15-5241 and 15-5170, respectively; photos by Nels Nelson. Fig. 6.4, courtesy Kent Lightfoot. Fig. 6.5, courtesy Tsim Schneider, photographer.

Chapter Seven: Fig. 7.1, courtesy Brian Codding, photographer. Figs. 7.2 and 7.3, courtesy National Anthropological Archives, Smithsonian Institution, nos. 91-31415 and 81-14072, respectively. Fig. 7.4, courtesy Roberta Greenwood, photographer. Fig. 7.5, prepared by Rusty van Rossmann. (Figs. 7.6 and 7.7 are in the public domain.)

Chapter Eight: Figs. 8.1, 8.5, 8.6, and 8.7, courtesy Michael Glassow, photographer. Fig. 8.2, map by Michael Glassow. Figs. 8.3 and 8.4, courtesy Jon Erlandson, photographer. Fig. 8.8, courtesy Robert Heizer Collection, Santa Barbara Museum of Natural History.

Chapter Nine: Fig. 9.1, courtesy University of California, Los Angeles, Department of Geography, Benjamin and Gladys Thomas Air Photo Archives, Spence Air Photo Collection. Figs. 9.2, 9.3, 9.4, 9.5, and 9.7, courtesy Statistical Research, Inc. Fig. 9.6, drawing by Luke Wisner, courtesy Statistical Research, Inc.

Chapter Ten: Fig. 10.1, courtesy Santa Barbara Museum of Natural History; photo by Leon de Cessac. Fig. 10.2, courtesy Honnold/Mudd Library Special Collections of the Claremont Colleges Library. Figs. 10.3 and 10.4, courtesy National Anthropological Archives, Smithsonian Institution; photos by A. W. Chase, 1874. Fig. 10.5, courtesy Lynn H. Gamble, photographer. Fig. 10.6, collection at the Repository for Archaeological and Ethnographic Collections, University of California, Santa Barbara; photo by Lynn H. Gamble. Fig. 10.7, courtesy Department of Anthropology, Smithsonian Institution, catalog no. A31383-0.

Chapter Eleven: Figs. 11.1 and 11.4, courtesy Santa Barbara Museum of Natural History. Fig. 11.2, courtesy National Museum of the American Indian, Smithsonian Institution acc. no. 7/6779; photo by Katherine Fogden. Fig. 11.3, collections of the Santa Barbara Museum of Natural History; photo by Lynn H. Gamble. Fig. 11.5, courtesy Brooklyn Museum, Museum Expedition 1906, Museum Collection Fund, 06.331.8076. Fig. 11.6, courtesy Phoebe A. Hearst Museum of Anthropology and Regents of the University of California, catalog no. 15-2682; photo by Samuel A. Barrett, 1906. Fig. 11.7, © 1965, California State Parks, courtesy California State Parks; Bill Pritchard, photographer.

Chapter Twelve: Fig. 12.1, courtesy Humboldt State University Library; photo by A. W. Ericson, about 1890. Fig. 12.2, courtesy Santa Barbara Museum of Natural History, cat. no. NA-CA-28-1C-2; photo by Lynn H. Gamble. Fig. 12.3, drawing by Chester King. Fig. 12.4, courtesy Fowler Museum at University of California, Los Angeles, cat. no. 524-2344; photo by Lynn H. Gamble. Fig. 12.5, courtesy Santa Barbara Museum of Natural History.

Chapter Thirteen: Fig. 13.1, photographed by R. A. Holmes, about 1876; image rephotographed for reproduction by William D. Hyder; reproduced by permission of the San Luis Obispo Historical Society. Figs. 13.2, 13.4, 13.5, 13.6, and 13.7, courtesy William D. Hyder, photographer. Fig. 13.3, drawing by Georgia Lee. Fig. 13.8, courtesy Rick Bury, photographer.

Chapter Fourteen: Figs. 14.1 and 14.7, courtesy Bancroft Library, University of California, Berkeley, 1963.002.1312-FR and 1977.021:12-AX. Fig. 14.2, map by Molly O'Halloran. Fig. 14.3, courtesy Karen Foster Wells, artist. Fig. 14.4, courtesy National Museum of the American Indian, Smithsonian Institution, cat. no. 063882; photo by Katherine Fogden. Fig. 14.5, courtesy California Department of Parks and Recreation. Fig. 14.6, courtesy John R. Johnson, photographer.

Chapter Fifteen: Fig. 15.1, published in Fr. Zephyrin Engelhardt, San Diego Mission (San Francisco: James H. Barry), 1920. Figs. 15.2, 15.4, and 15.7, courtesy Tsim Schneider, photographer. Fig. 15.3, courtesy Getty Research Institute, Los Angeles, 85-B5605. Fig. 15.5, courtesy University of Southern California on behalf of the USC Libraries Special Collections. Fig. 15.6, published in Fr. Zephyrin Engelhardt, Santa Barbara Mission (San Francisco: James H. Barry), 1923.

Chapter Sixteen: Fig. 16.1, courtesy Jon Erlandson, photographer. Figs. 16.2, 16.3, and 16.4, courtesy William E. Kendig, photographer.

Chapter Seventeen: Fig. 17.1, courtesy Vera Powers, photographer. Figs. 17.2 and 17.3, courtesy Linda Yamane, photographer. Figs. 17.4 and 17.6, courtesy Tim Thomas, photographer. Fig. 17.5, courtesy National Anthropological Archives, Smithsonian Institution, catalog no. 313234; photo by Linda Yamane.

Index

Page numbers in *italics* refer to illustrations.